Supreme Folly

W · W · NORTON & COMPANY · NEW YORK · LONDON

Supreme Folly

RODNEY R. JONES

and

GERALD F. UELMEN

The text of this book is composed in Avanta, with the display set in Mistral and
Spectra Heavy. Composition and manufacturing by the Haddon Craftsmen, Inc.

First published as a Norton paperback 1993

Library of Congress Cataloging-in-Publication Data
Jones, Rodney R.
Supreme folly / by Rodney R. Jones and Gerald F. Uelmen.
p. cm.
1. Trials—United States—Humor. I. Uelmen, Gerald F.
II. Title.
K184.J665 1990
347.73'7'0207—dc20
[347.30770207]   89–77776

ISBN 0-393-30941-X

W.W. Norton & Company, Inc., 500 Fifth Avenue, New York, N.Y. 10110
W.W. Norton & Company Ltd, 10 Coptic Street, London WC1A 1PU

2 3 4 5 6 7 8 9 0

CONTENTS

FOREWORD

In *Disorderly Conduct*, we mined the "pits" of trial court transcripts for humorous exchanges. With *Supreme Folly*, we briefly revisit the trial courts, then move up the judicial ladder to the appellate courts. The difference is significant. As Judge Irving Kaufman once put it, trial courts are engaged in a search for the truth while appellate courts are engaged in a search for error. Trial courts decide questions of fact, through the presentation of witnesses and exhibits to judges and juries. Appellate courts decide questions of law, based on written arguments presented in lawyers' briefs. The judges write their decisions in published opinions. Those opinions provide some of the fodder for this collection of judicial wit. The rest was supplied by fragments from the refuse of our "litigation explosion."

The wit found in appellate decisions tends to be deliberate and premeditated. The lack of spontaneity is more than offset, however, by literary flair. The craft of appellate judges is the precise use of words. While low humor abounds in the high courts, it is frequently served with the thrust of a razor.

Many lawyers and judges permitted us to raid their

personal collections for this material. We are especially grateful to Judge H. Sol Clark (Retired) of Savannah, Georgia; attorney Kent Bridwell of Los Angeles, California; attorney and author Charles Sevilla of San Diego, California; Justice Rudolph Gerber of Arizona; Justice Arthur Gilbert of Ventura, California; Bankruptcy Judge Stanley B. Bernstein of Detroit, Michigan; Tax Court Judge William Fay and attorney Jacob Stein of Washington, D.C.; attorney Robert J. Lifton of Chicago, Illinois; Judge A. Jay Cristol of Florida; and barrister Richard Burns of Leicester, England.

We are deeply indebted to Jackie Collins and Carole Vendrick for turning a cut-and-paste mess into a presentable manuscript, to our editor Hilary Hinzmann, whose encouragement and good taste are reflected throughout, and to Tom Brinley and Peter Viano, Santa Clara Law School '90, for tracking down citations. Those who don't believe this stuff actually came out of officially reported opinions will find citations collected in the Table of Cases at the back of the book.

Rodney R. Jones
Gerald F. Uelmen

Supreme Folly

1

OBJECTIONS
OVERRULED

"Where is the evidence that doth accuse me?
What lawful quest have given their verdict up
Unto the frowning judge?"
WILLIAM SHAKESPEARE, RICHARD III (I, iv, 186)

It was in Winslow, Arizona, and the year was 1908. Justice of the Peace Waltron was presiding over a case involving a $22 plumbing bill, with oral advocacy by U.S. Senator (and attorney) Henry Ashurst:

MR. ASHURST Your Honor, as I approached the trial of this case today, my heart was burdened with crushing and gloomy forebodings. The immense responsibility of my client's welfare bowed me down with apprehensions. A cold fear gripped my heart as I dwelt upon the possibility that, through some oversight or shortcoming of mine, there might ensue dreadful consequences to my client, and I shrank within myself as the ordeal became more imminent.

Yet the nearer my uncertain steps brought me to this tribunal of justice, distinguished as it has been for years as the one court of the rugged West where fame attended the wisdom and justice of the decisions of Your Honor, a serene confidence came to my troubled emotions, and the raging waters of tumultuous floods that had surged hotly but a moment before were stilled. Your Honor, I was no longer appalled. I no longer feared the issue in this case.

Aye, I reflected that throughout the long years of your administration as judge, there had grown up here a halo as it were of honor and glory illumining Your Honor's record, eloquent of a fame that will augment with the flight of years and with increasing luster light the pathway of humanity down the ages so long as the heaving billows of the stormy Mediterranean shall beat vainly upon the cliffs of Gibraltar . . .

JUSTICE WALTRON   Sit down, Mr. Ashurst. You can't blow any smoke up this court's ass.

. . . .

An Oklahoma man, charged with armed robbery, elected to defend himself. He handled his case well until the store manager identified him as the robber, at which point the defendant leaped to his feet, accused the woman of lying, and exclaimed, "I should have blown your f—— head off." He then paused, sat down, and muttered, "If I'd been the one that was there."

. . . .

THE COURT   Any other motions?
DEFENDANT   Yes, I do, Your Honor. Here's a motion—this is not trying to be sarcastic or anything but I have no other way to present my defense. It's a motion for a homing pigeon, Your Honor.
THE COURT   Motion for a homing pigeon?
DEFENDANT   Yes, Your Honor. This way at least I'll be able to communicate with the court. You won't allow me stamps, you won't allow

me any other means. I figure that wouldn't put such a financial burden on the court.

THE COURT   All right, the court has received a four-page handwritten document entitled "Motion for Homing Pigeon and Pigeon Supplies." You're asking for a pair of homing pigeons?

DEFENDANT   Yeah, Your Honor. That's just in case one of them gets hung up on the way or something. I have a back-up.

THE COURT   And a 50-pound bag of pigeon seed?

DEFENDANT   Yes, Your Honor. I think it's a very appropriate motion considering Your Honor has denied me every other means to provide an adequate defense.

THE COURT   And you want the court to provide anti–pigeon-drip clothing?

DEFENDANT   Yes, Your Honor.

THE COURT   What is that?

DEFENDANT   Well, maybe perhaps a raincoat, Your Honor.

THE COURT   A raincoat?

DEFENDANT   Yeah.

THE COURT   For the pigeon?

DEFENDANT   Well, yeah, for the pigeon drops.

THE COURT   And you're also asking for one expert pigeon trainer?

DEFENDANT   Yes, Your Honor. I don't know anything about pigeons.

THE COURT   And one small message pouch and a pigeon foot attachment?

DEFENDANT   Yes, Your Honor.

THE COURT   Must be the peanuts I had for lunch. And
               you want four rolls of paper towels?

DEFENDANT   Yes, Your Honor.

THE COURT   To wipe off protective eyewear in case of
               an emergency pigeon landing on forehead?

DEFENDANT   Yes, Your Honor.

THE COURT   Do you have any authority for these
               items?

DEFENDANT   No, Your Honor. But any authority I
               presented to the court thus far hasn't
               worked. And I don't have any way to
               contact my witnesses or, you know, put on
               an adequate defense, Your Honor.

THE COURT   You have a very fine sense of humor, sir.

               . . . .

PROSECUTOR   As a result of the conversation with Rico
               did you take a photograph?

WITNESS   Yes.

PROSECUTOR   And could you tell the court what that
               photograph was of?

WITNESS   His penis.

PROSECUTOR   Detective, is that the photograph you took
               that day?

WITNESS   Yes.

THE COURT   Well, did you cause this photograph to be
               taken?

WITNESS   Yes, I did.

THE COURT   The hand that is shown holding the penis,
               is that your hand?

WITNESS   Ah . . . [inaudible]
               . . .

THE COURT   Yes, well, this does add some humor to
               this case, but I'm concerned with the best
               way to determine whether this photograph
               can be admitted into evidence. Although
               it is clearly a photograph of a penis, it
               could be one that belongs to someone else.
               I suppose what I can do is order an
               independent examination to compare the
               defendant's penis to the one shown in the
               photograph to make sure that we are
               concerned with the same penis. I realize
               that such an examination will be
               somewhat embarrassing, but I have no
               other choice. Is Court Officer H. here?

A.   Yes, here.

THE COURT   Mr. H., we have a difficult situation here.
               It involves the genuineness of this
               photograph. We are going to have to
               make a comparison between this
               photograph and the defendant's penis to
               make sure we are talking about the same
               penis. Would you be able to carry that out?

OFFICER H.   I guess so.

THE COURT   All right. Please carry out your duty and
               be prepared to testify before the jury as to
               whether the penis you observe in the
               men's room is the same one shown in this
               photograph, keeping in mind size, texture,
               quality, and so on. We'll take a brief
               recess and await word from Mr. H.

                    . . .

THE COURT   The record may indicate that it was not
               necessary for Mr. H. to make a full and

"If it please the Court, I move that these snores be stricken from the record."

complete comparison. Counsel have agreed
that the penis shown in the photograph is
in fact the penis of the defendant. Is that
correct, Counsel?

COUNSEL　Yes, Your Honor.

THE COURT　Hopefully, we have saved some
embarrassment to the defendant, and
prevented Mr. H. from carrying out his
duty as a penis examiner.

．．．．．．．．．．．．．．

PROSECUTOR　Could you describe how the fatal blows
were inflicted?

WITNESS　Well, first the defendant hit him with his
right hand to the left side of his face, then
he hit him again with the left hand to the
right side of his face.

PROSECUTOR　And then?

WITNESS　Then he repeated the blows a second
time, right to left side of face, left to right
side. You know . . . the defendant is one
of those guys who is amphibious.

．．．．．．．．．．．．．．

COUNSEL　Who was that?

WITNESS　Melinda.

COUNSEL　Do you know Melinda's last name? Is
there something about Melinda that stands
out?

WITNESS　She's got big breasts.

. . . .

DEFENSE COUNSEL   Okay, how long did you work for J. C.
                 Penney's and what did you do there?
      WITNESS   Oh . . . almost four months. I was a BRC
                 . . . a bin replenishing clerk.
DEFENSE COUNSEL   Basically, what is that?
      WITNESS   Well, you replenish bins.

. . . .

   PROSECUTOR   Now, you have described McKenna and
                 Pacheco as throwing firecrackers at you?
       VICTIM   Yes. They put one in my ear.
   PROSECUTOR   Did that explode?
       VICTIM   Pardon?

. . . .

   During a noon recess of the defendant's trial on a
charge of resisting arrest, the judge attended the annual
Christmas luncheon of the Dallas Bar Association. On
his return, the judge announced to the jury: "Ladies
and Gentlemen, I have just been to dinner and I believe I have eaten more than I have eaten in my life and
if I go to sleep up here, you whistle at me, will you?"
The prosecutor resumed cross-examination. When the
defense lawyer made an objection, he couldn't rouse
the judge for a ruling. On appeal, the conviction was
affirmed despite the judge's nap. The court of appeals
concluded he hadn't missed much anyway.
Jackson v. State, Texas Court of Criminal Appeals
(1982)

. . . .

COUNSEL	Throughout the morning I noticed you raising your eyebrows and smiling at some of the answers in disbelief, exhibiting to me at least facial expressions of disbelief.
THE COURT	It's incredible, absolutely incredible.
COUNSEL	I know. I'm sorry to have to say this. Would you prefer to go into chambers?
THE COURT	No. Go on.
COUNSEL	I noticed you and the clerk looking at each other, raising your eyebrows and smiling during some of the testimony, and it puts me in a terrible position to make a motion for a mistrial and then we have this exchange.
THE COURT	This exchange is nothing. I expect the witness to be able to answer a question without that—she answered it, didn't she? The motion is denied. I want it noted that during a trial I am generally conducting more things than just the trial. There are other things here, including cases that I am citing, and so on, and there are numerous messages passed between the clerk and myself that have nothing to do whatsoever with the trial.

. . . .

PROSECUTOR	You have sinned, have you not, Mr. Featherstone?
DEFENDANT	At one time, before my conversion.

PROSECUTOR   You have sinned by breaking people's bones, haven't you?

DEFENDANT   Before my conversion, yes.

PROSECUTOR   You have plunged knives into people, have you not?

DEFENDANT   Before my conversion, yes.

PROSECUTOR   You have shot at people, have you not?

DEFENDANT   Before my conversion.

PROSECUTOR   Have you killed anybody, Mr. Featherstone?

DEFENDANT   Beg your pardon?

PROSECUTOR   Have you killed anybody?

DEFENDANT   I take the Fifth on that.

. . . .

ATTORNEY   Did you stay all night with this man in New York?

WITNESS   I refuse to answer that question.

ATTORNEY   Did you stay all night with this man in Chicago?

WITNESS   I refuse to answer that question.

ATTORNEY   Did you stay all night with this man in Miami?

WITNESS   No.

. . . .

The defendant, on trial for the murder of a prison kitchen supervisor, objected to his public defender's refusal to call some witnesses. During a conference in the judge's chambers, the defendant struck the public defender over the head with a chair, and then punched the judge on the head with his fist. The defendant was shackled, and the trial continued, resulting in his conviction. On appeal, he objected to the failure of the judge and public defender to disqualify themselves, because they might have been prejudiced against him after he assaulted them. The objection was overruled. *People v. Hall,* Illinois Supreme Court (1986)

. . . .

During closing argument in an armed robbery case, the prosecutor produced a suspicious-smelling paper bag. He said to the jury, "I told you I thought the defense lawyer was throwing out a lot of red herrings in this case. About halfway through this trial I believe that you sensed something smelled funny here. That's what the smell is coming from," he announced, as he opened the bag and pulled out a board on which a pile of cow manure was neatly mounted.

. . . .

In *Epple v. State* (Texas, 1929), the defendant, sentenced to three years in the state penitentiary for bootlegging, objected that he was not granted a continuance to locate a missing witness:

The main fact which appellant proposed to prove by this absent witness was that there was no whiskey in the car in question when appellant and witness left it to go in a restaurant, and that, on coming out of the restaurant a short

"Effective, but I prefer the more traditional gavel."

while thereafter and just before the search, witness saw an unknown stranger in the car, who suddenly left; that he did not know where he went and had never seen him before. The appellant's theory seems to have been that this stranger had in some way found a mysteriously hidden receptacle in the upholstering of his car and played him the mean trick of filling it with whiskey. Like a cuckoo bird, this unfeathered follower of Bacchus surreptitiously slipped a whole settin' of eggs into appellant's nest, after which he was apparently swallowed up by space, leaving his troublesome brood to be hatched by another. We believe in Santa Claus all right, but we confess the increasingly frequent appearance of this same stranger in whiskey cases inclines us to relegate him to the mythical realm of Dido and Aeneas. This ubiquitous disciple of John Barleycorn seems to have a peculiar habit of hovering around places just prior to their raid and search by officers, and then as mysteriously evaporating as the mists of an April morning. Unlike the roaring lion seeking whom he may devour, this omnipresent individual moves with the silent tread of a fairy and the swiftness of the lightning stroke, and over practically the entire state there have come complaints from his victims.

. . . .

In a Missouri fraud trial, the defendant complained that the following argument of plaintiff's counsel was "inflammatory, prejudicial, unethical and untrue":

You may remember when Christ was preaching the Gospel, in the Holy Roman Empire, that Julius Caesar was the Emperor of Rome. As Christ was making his way toward Rome, the Mennonites and the Philistines stopped him in the road and they sought to entrap him. They asked Christ: "Shall we continue to pay tribute unto Caesar?" And you will remember, in the Book of St. Matthew it is written that Christ said: "Render ye unto Caesar the things that are Caesar's and unto God the things that are God's."

Although it concluded the errors did not require reversal, the court found the argument contained an "abundance of misinformation":

The Holy Roman Empire did not come into existence until about 800 years after Christ. Julius Caesar, who was never Emperor of Rome, was dead before Christ was born. Christ was never on his way to Rome and the Philistines had disappeared from Palestine before the birth of Christ. The Mennonites are a devout Protestant sect that arose in the sixteenth century A.D. This phrase is noteworthy only because of the ease with which the speaker crowded into one short paragraph such an abundance of misinformation. It is not, however, even pendulously attached to the argument following, which deals with taking from Brookshire and rendering unto Hall.

Hall v. Brookshire, Missouri Supreme Court (1955)

. . . .

A judge unhappy with a state supreme court ruling that drunks should not be jailed had police deliver two men charged with drunkenness to the supreme court building.

The Charleston, West Virginia, municipal court judge said he was responding to the state supreme court's recent ruling that it was "cruel and unusual punishment" to jail chronic drunks. The court gave authorities one year to end the practice.

"I consider that being partially pregnant," the judge said. "Either it's constitutional [to jail drunks] or not."

He shipped the two men, who had appeared before him several times before for being drunk, to the high court "because they have more facilities at the state to handle this than we do."

The action drew mixed comment from the justices, who never saw the pair. As for the two men themselves? They hesitated only seconds after supreme court clerk George Singleton told them they were free to leave without spending a night in the slammer.

One court worker said one of the men kept looking over his shoulder and asking, "Are you sure it's okay for us to go?"

. . . .

A defense attorney said he would appeal his client's conviction, charging that the prosecutor disrupted the four-week trial by repeatedly passing gas.

"It was disgusting," said Clark Head, a Calaveras County lawyer representing a burglary defendant.

Head said he was considering basing the appeal, in part, on "misconduct" by the Tuolumne County district attorney.

Head said the prosecutor passed gas "about 100 times. He even lifted his leg several times."

Head said he went on the record to protest the tactic after the prosecutor passed gas during the defense's closing argument. His objection was overruled.

. . . .

The defendant was a middle-aged male Greek immi-
grant who had recently come to the United States. He
was charged with running a stop sign and disorderly
conduct. His opening remark to the judge was, "Your
Honor, what means 'fuck you'?" The judge's jaw
dropped in disbelief. The defendant said it again. The
judge got angry and demanded to know what this
meant. The defendant went on to explain that his
American friends told him that if a police officer stops
him, he should say, "Fuck you." He continued his explanation by saying he was stopped by a police officer
and did what his friends had suggested. After telling
this to the judge, he repeated, "Your Honor, what
means 'fuck you'?" After hysterical courtroom laughter
subsided, the judge dismissed both charges.

. . . .

Federal District Judge Edward R. Becker has proposed utilizing the "Time Out" rule to accelerate the
pace of slow-moving litigation. He spelled out the following statement of the rule in an appendix to his opinion in *Zenith Radio Corp. v. Matsushita Elec. Indus.
Co.:*

"Time Out" Rule
For no good cause shown* each side will be entitled to
three (3) time outs between now and the date of trial. A

---

*"No good cause shown" is defined as family events, such as anniversaries, birth-
days, sporting events involving siblings, laziness, genuine ennui (pronounced *nue*),
drunkenness, firm events such as annual dinner dance or outing, and anything else
which helps attorneys to keep their sanity during the course of these proceedings.

time out is defined as a one-week period in which no discovery can be served, all deadlines are postponed, and counsel can generally goof off.

The procedure for calling a time out will be as follows: Both plaintiffs and defendants will designate one individual as the official time-out person (hereinafter referred to as the "Designated Whistler"). The designated whistler will be issued a whistle from the case liaison logistics committee which will be strung around his, her, or its neck. When a time out is desired, the designated whistler will go to the offices of opposing lead counsel (see paragraph XVI.E.) and blow the whistle three (3) times. Thereafter there will a one (1) week time out.

. . . .

2

TRIAL BY JURY

"The jury, passing on the prisoner's life,
May in the sworn twelve have a thief or two
Guiltier than him they try."
              WILLIAM SHAKESPEARE, MEASURE FOR
                                    MEASURE (II, i, 19)

"A juror is not some kind of a dithering nincompoop, brought
in from never-never land and exposed to the harsh realities of life
for the first time in the jury box."
        JUSTICE ROBERT GARDNER, PEOPLE V. LONG

THE COURT	What is a jury trial?
DEFENDANT	I don't know.
THE COURT	Give it a guess; what do you think it is?
DEFENDANT	They all come together and kick back, some on one side, some on the other, I don't know.
THE COURT	I like that. Where they all come together and kick back, some on one side and some on the other. One better than that is where they hear the evidence, slap you around a little bit, find you guilty. That is the one I sort of like.

. . . .

An undercover narcotics police officer, testifying before a New York City grand jury, looked out at the jurors. In the second row, he recognized a suspect he had bought narcotics from a month before. After the officer left the grand jury room, he rushed to find a prosecutor. A day later, a 23-year-old grand juror was quietly taken out of the jury room and arrested. He was later indicted for felony sale of narcotics—but not by the same grand jury on which he had been sitting.

. . . .

A juror in Wichita, Kansas thought the defendant on trial looked familiar. "I kept looking at him, and I knew I knew him, but I just couldn't place him." Finally, she told the bailiff that she thought he might be the same man she convicted while sitting on a jury six years before. The next day, she was told it was indeed the same man, and she was excused from the jury.

. . . .

Wayne County, Michigan Circuit Judge Charles Kaufman kept a straight face as he asked a potential juror whether she knew any of the participants in the proceeding. "Yes, I'm your wife," the juror replied. After receiving her assurance she could still be fair and impartial, neither side moved to strike her as a juror for a malpractice case.

. . . .

Georgia lawyer Bobby Lee Cook was representing a defendant charged with shooting a man who had called him "a goddamn son of a bitch." The prosecutor told the jury that being called "a goddamn son of a bitch" wasn't a real reason to shoot a man over—maybe hitting him a time or two, but not shooting him.

Bobby Lee got up in front of the jury and started telling the jury how the victim was really "one mean dude that the police are glad is gone." He got on a roll and noticed some of the jurors even nodding their heads in agreement. He looked at the jury and said, "What if he had called you a goddamn son of a bitch?" An older gentleman sitting on the back row of the jury box stood up and said, "Why I'da killed the goddamn son of a bitch."

The jury acquitted.

. . . .

During the years of English rule in Ireland, a man was brought before an English judge on a charge of stealing a cow. After the jury was sworn, the prisoner was brought in and the judge realized he was not represented by counsel. The judge said, "I must tell you that you are charged with a very serious offense, and if convicted you may be sent to prison for a considerable time. Surely you have at least a solicitor to say something for you?" "Not a soul, me lord," replied the prisoner. "But I've several good friends among the jury."

. . . .

In 1882, the California Supreme Court was presented with an appeal by a defendant convicted of murder who complained that the jury deliberating his fate had consumed 20 gallons of beer, two casks of wine, and two bottles of whiskey, as well as other wine and whiskey at each meal, including breakfast. The conviction was reversed and the case was remanded for a new trial in a drier location.
People v. Gray, California Supreme Court (1882)

. . . .

Until a century ago, there was no such thing as a "hung jury." The law required that jurors be kept "without food, drink, fire, or candle" until they reached a verdict. The result: few "hung" juries, but many hungry ones.

· · · · · · · · · · · · · · ·

After the jurors spent three and a half days deliberating the fate of a defendant accused of robbing a grocery store, the California judge presiding at the trial called jurors in and told them that because of the limitations on fiscal expenditures imposed by a tax-cutting initiative, the court would no longer pay for their lunch. They would be free to separate for lunch on their own, then resume deliberations after lunch. The jurors promptly returned to the jury room and unanimously agreed on a verdict of guilty.

People v. Guerrero, California Court of Appeal (1979)

· · · · · · · · · · · · · · ·

During the long conspiracy trial of *United States v. Beltempo* in the Federal Court in Brooklyn, New York, one of the jurors wrote a love letter to the female prosecutor, inviting her to lunch or dinner. He enclosed a picture of himself and a poem. The prosecutor turned the letter over to the trial judge, who concluded the best thing to do was simply ignore it. On appeal, the court of appeals agreed. They concluded, "No recognized ground is presented to impeach the verdict on this issue."

Another female prosecutor was the object of unwanted attention during the fraud trial of *United States v. Widgery* in federal court in Arkansas. Defense counsel claimed a male juror was "blowing kisses, winking and waving" at the prosecutor. The court ruled that a mistrial was not warranted, especially since counsel waited until after alternate jurors were excused before voicing his objection.

. . . .

While the jury was being selected for her trial on fraud charges, the attractive defendant was observed mouthing her telephone number to a juror who had been "making eyes" at her. The juror was excused. Later, the prosecutor complained that the defendant called him at 1:00 A.M. and told him "she had a crush on him and wanted to be with him." The judge announced that he would revoke defendant's bail and jail her during the trial. But after a conference with the defendant and her attorney, the judge announced he had a "change of heart" and would allow the defendant to remain free on bail.

. . . .

THE COURT   Well, Ms., I was told by our courtroom
             deputy, and my law clerk, James, that you
             inquired as to whether the defendants
             were out on bail or in custody. Did you
             make that inquiry?
JUROR   Yes.
THE COURT   What was the reason?
JUROR   Because one of the defendants has hickeys
             on his neck. I noticed it yesterday, so I
             was just wondering.

. . . .

In *Central Railroad of Banking Co. of Georgia v. Roberts,* the defendant complained that a stepdaughter of one of the jurors was going to marry the plaintiff's brother. In rejecting this complaint, the court explored the legal depths of this relationship:

Marriage will relate the husband, by affinity, to the wife's blood relations, but will not relate the husband's brother to any of her relations. The husband of the juror's stepdaughter was not related to the juror, but only to the juror's wife. The husband's brother, the plaintiff, was further off still. He was not related even to the juror's wife.

> *The groom and bride each comes within*
> *The circle of the other's kin;*
> *But kin and kin are still no more*
> *Related than they were before.*

. . . .

During the selection of a jury for a first degree murder trial in Madison County, Indiana, challenges were allowed to dismiss 50 out of 60 prospective jurors. The judge ordered the sheriff to find some more jury prospects. Police operated a roadblock until they found 15 eligible county residents. Two of the motorists were seated on the jury.

. . . .

THE COURT   I have a communiqué from the jury.
DEFENSE COUNSEL   Number Four again?

"Your Honor, my client demands to be tried by a jury of his peers."

THE COURT   I heard this sort of rumble over there
             earlier this afternoon and the jurors sort of
             looked strange.
                 Well, it seems for the last week and a half
             he has been passing gas like mad in the jury
             box, and the jurors are rather upset about it.
DEFENSE COUNSEL   I don't know if we need this on the
             record—
THE COURT   This has been going on for a week and a
             half. A couple of them asked if their seats
             can be moved, but there are only so many
             seats in the box and he is right in the
             middle.
                 I don't know whether we can seat him
             somewhere across the room or something—
DEFENSE COUNSEL   Shall we go off the record.
THE COURT   All right.
                 (Discussion off the record.)
THE COURT   Counsel have agreed that we will resume
             for the next half an hour today, finish out
             the day, and at the end of the day the
             clerk will excuse Juror Number Four and
             tomorrow morning we will sit an alternate.
MR. K   I agree.
DEFENSE COUNSEL   So stipulated.

. . . .

A defendant convicted of rape in Richland County,
South Carolina, complained that the jury that tried
him conducted an illegal experiment to check key evidence in his case.
    The victim had testified she bit her assailant on the

arm during the attack, but could not identify the defendant.

The prosecution relied on police photographs of a bruise on one of the defendant's arms when he was arrested and on a doctor's testimony that the bruise was caused by human teeth.

The defendant claimed he was bruised when he scraped his arm on a chain-link fence the night of the rape.

The jury, in trying to make up its mind, conducted an experiment in which a woman juror bit the foreman's arm.

The jurors then made periodic checks on the resulting bruise and compared it with the photos of the defendant's arm.

On appeal, the resulting conviction was upheld. The court concluded the "bizarre and painful experiment" did not prejudice the jury.

. . . .

A Southern California jury was deadlocked on deciding a drug case. One of the jurors prayed to God that the single hold-out juror would change his vote to guilty. If her prayers were to be answered, he would arrive the next day dressed in a blue blazer as a sign from God. He did and the defendant was convicted. The defendant has since appealed, arguing that the prayerful juror was not able to give serious consideration to the views of dissenting jurors once she was convinced her vote was divinely inspired.

. . . .

3

FRIVOLOUS
QUESTIONS

"Good Lord, what madness rules in brainsick men,
When for so slight and frivolous a cause
Such factious emulations shall arise!"
    WILLIAM SHAKESPEARE, 1 HENRY VI (IV, i, 111)

Each of the questions which follow was posed in an actual case presented in a court of law. The "holding" is the ruling of the court which can be cited as a "precedent" in future cases.

. . . .

Are communications with God protected against electronic eavesdropping or wiretapping?

The defendant, accused of arson in setting forest fires, was brought to the headquarters of the Royal Canadian Mounted Police to take a lie detector test. He was not told the room was fitted with a concealed television camera and microphone. While alone waiting for the test to begin, he slid out of his chair, got down on his knees, put his arms in the air, and said, "Oh God, let me get away with it just this once." At his trial, a videotape of his prayer was offered in evidence. The defendant argued that the recording violated a Canadian law prohibiting the interception of private communications "made under circumstances in which it is reasonable for the originator thereof to expect that it will not be intercepted by any person other than the person intended by the originator thereof to receive it." The prosecutor argued that only communications to other "persons" are included, and God is not a "person" within the meaning of the law.

HELD   ". . . The word 'person' is used in the statutes of Canada to describe someone to whom rights are granted and upon whom obligations are placed. There is no earthly authority which can grant rights or impose

duties upon God. I can find no reason to
think that the Parliament of Canada has
attempted to do so . . ." The videotape
was admitted in evidence.
Regina v. Davie, British Columbia Court of
Appeal

. . . .

Is living in Iowa cruel and unusual punishment?

The defendant was paroled from federal prison on
condition he live in Sioux City, Iowa, and not leave the
federal district of northern Iowa for twelve years. He
asked the court to set aside the condition he remain in
Iowa as "cruel and unusual punishment," so he could
return to Seattle.

HELD   "Although we might share Bagley's
enthusiasm for the Pacific Northwest, we
believe, and so hold, that it is not cruel
and unusual punishment to require Bagley
to serve his parole term in Iowa."
Bagley v. Harvey, U.S. Court of Appeals for
the Ninth Circuit

. . . .

Is a marshmallow a deadly weapon?

Two youths were arrested on Halloween for firing
miniature marshmallows from slingshots. They were
charged with the felony offense of assault with a deadly
weapon. They sought to have the charges reduced to a
misdemeanor.

HELD "None of the victims of the assault were hit with anything harder than a soft marshmallow, shot at a distance with slow speed over the heads of the victims, which popped down and hit the victims on the head. That would be a misdemeanor battery at most."
People v. Callendar and Krasomil, Los Angeles County Superior Court

. . . .

Does a pregnant woman, driving alone, qualify as a "car pool"?

California freeways frequently reserve a special lane for car pools and buses during rush hours, posting signs which warn, "A car pool requires two or more persons occupying the vehicle." The defendant was ticketed for driving alone in the car pool lane during rush hours. When she appeared in court, obviously pregnant, she contended that her unborn child was a "person," therefore she qualified as a "car pool." The prosecution protested that police officers were in no position to confirm the validity of a driver's claim she was pregnant, suggesting, "A woman could stuff pillows up her dress."

HELD An unborn child is a person for purposes of forming a two-person car pool.
People v. Yaeger, Orange County Municipal Court

. . . .

Life in the fast lane was rejected, however, for the driver of a mortuary van. The driver claimed that four frozen cadavers he was transporting qualified his vehicle for the car pool lane. Orange County Municipal Court Judge Richard Stanford, Jr., ruled that passengers must be alive to qualify.

People v. Hanshew, Orange County Municipal Court

. . . .

Are a family of four, asleep in their beds at home, pedestrians?

Defendant, on her way home from a party, drove her car through a wall of plaintiffs' home. The car came to rest in one of the children's bedrooms at 1:30 A.M. When the plaintiffs sued for damages, the defendant argued that the action was covered by the limitations of the Colorado No-Fault Act, which included all accidents sustained by "pedestrians."

HELD Pedestrians include only persons on or about public roadways, not those who are home in bed.

Smith v. Simpson, Colorado Court of Appeals

. . . .

Is a hamburger a sandwich?

A Long Island shopping center owner entered a rental agreement with a Blimpie Sandwich Shop. The lease provided that Blimpie was to be the only "sandwich shop" in the shopping center. Several months later, the owner leased another shop in the same center to Wendy's Old-Fashioned Hamburgers. When Blimpie protested, the owner argued that the lease was not violated, because Wendy's only sold hamburgers, not "sandwiches."

> HELD   A hamburger is defined in the dictionary as "a sandwich made with a patty of ground beef, usually in a round bun." Therefore, a hamburger shop is a sandwich shop.
> *Blimpie's v. S. & E. Realty Corp.*, New York Supreme Court

· · · · · · · · · · · · · · ·

Is revocation of a woman's driver's license an excessive penalty for deliberately running over her husband?

The petitioner protested the revocation of her driver's license by the Commissioner of Motor Vehicles as excessive punishment. Testimony revealed that after petitioner and her new husband left their wedding reception, her husband got out of the car, lay down in front of it, and told her to run over him. The dutiful wife did so, inflicting fatal injuries.

> HELD   The revocation of her driver's license was not so severe as to be shocking to one's sense of justice. She could apply for a new driver's license after 30 days.
> *Bonitatibus v. Melton,* New York Supreme Court

"And will you tell the jury where your legs were on the night of January 12th?"

. . . .

Can an insurance claimant be his own grandpaw?

The stepson of the driver of an automobile involved in a crash sought to recover for injuries under his stepfather's insurance policy. The policy excluded from coverage "driver relatives under the age of 25." The insurance company contended that a "stepson" is a "relative." The court noted,

"I'm my own grandpaw" ran the rollicking refrain reciting a litany of the consanguinal complications created by a hillbilly's marriage to a widow when his father entered into a nuptial union with the widow's daughter. This popular ditty of the twenties comes to mind in seeking to solve the legal question presented in the instant case: Is a stepson a relative of his stepfather?

HELD   Although dictionary definitions of "relative" include affines as well as consanguines, embracing kin, kith, kinfold, and kindred, the word cannot carry such an all-inclusive generic meaning in every instance. The stepson was allowed to recover.
Southeastern Fidelity Ins. Co. v. Fluellen

. . . .

Is a woman's cleavage an "intimate part"?

The Oregon Criminal Code prohibits unconsented touching of "the sexual or other intimate parts" of another person. The defendant, convicted of touching between the victim's breasts without her consent, contended this was not an "intimate part." The court noted that "subjective and cultural differences" might affect what parts of the body are considered intimate:

Are lips intimate parts? Are knees or feet intimate, hands or elbows not? To hold that these are or are not intimate parts as a matter of law assumes that the lawmakers had in mind a chart or catalogue of "intimate" parts, which they did not list in the law but expect courts to divine from the word itself.

HELD　Whether a part is "intimate" must be left to the jury in each case, under instructions to apply a "two prong" test, measuring the subjective expectations of the victim and the objective reasonableness of the defendant's belief.
State v. Woodley, Oregon Supreme Court

. . . .

Is a girdle a "burglar's tool"?

Defendant was observed by security guards at Macy's department store dropping various items inside her girdle. She was charged with possession of a "burglar's tool."

HELD　Declaring a girdle to be a "burglar's tool" would stretch the plain meaning of the prohibition of possession of such tools.

The Court has decided this issue mindful of the heavy burden that a contrary decision would place upon retail merchants. Thus is avoided the real bind of having customers check not only packages, but their girdles too, at the department store's door. The court must also wonder whether such a contrary decision would not create a spate of unreasonable bulges that would let loose the floodgate of stop and frisk cases, with the result of putting the squeeze on court resources already overextended in this era of trim governmental budgets.
In the Matter of Charlotte K., Richmond County Family Court, New York

. . . .

Do you become a year older on your birthday?

The defendant was charged with the commission of a crime the day before his 18th birthday. The prosecution charged him as an adult, relying on three court decisions saying that since you complete a year's existence on the day *before* your birthday, you become a year older on that day.

HELD   You age a year on your birthday, and not a day sooner. The prior decisions were overruled, and the defendant was tried as a juvenile.
Johnson v. Superior Court, California Court of Appeal

. . . .

Can you sue yourself?

In an action "to quiet [settle] title" filed on his own behalf, the plaintiff named himself as a defendant, then had a default judgment entered against himself when he failed to answer the complaint. When the judgment was dismissed, he appealed, filing briefs on both sides.

HELD   The complaint was properly dismissed.
           In the circumstances this result cannot be unfair to Mr. Lodi. Although it is true that as plaintiff and appellant he loses, it is equally true that as defendant and respondent, he wins! It is hard to imagine a more even-handed application of justice. Truly it would appear that Oreste Lodi is that rare litigant who is assured of both victory and defeat regardless of which side triumphs.
           Lodi v. Lodi, California Court of Appeal

. . . .

Is the solicitation of four murders one crime or four?

The defendant was convicted of four separate solicitation of murder charges. On appeal, he argued that since the solicitations all occurred at the same time and place, they should be treated as one offense.

HELD   Since the solicitations were not a "lump sum deal," the defendant would have to

take his lumps one at a time. All four
convictions were affirmed.
Meyer v. State, Maryland Court of Special
Appeals

. . . .

Are nude cookies obscene?

An Annapolis bakery was selling the traditional gin-
gerbread man with "discernible sex organs." Local
Moral Majority leaders mounted a "ban the cookie"
crusade, and sought to persuade the local prosecutor to
file charges under a state law prohibiting the sale of
nude pictures to minors. They actually sent two minors
into the bakery "under cover" to purchase the offending cookies. The minors reported that the bakery did
not ask for their identifications to verify their ages
before making the sale.

HELD   This one never got to court. The
prosecutor declined prosecution,
commenting that it was a "crumby case."

. . . .

*Is death during a sexual tryst with a co-worker a
"work-related injury"?*

A project engineer for a Michigan automotive company was assigned to work at a British subsidiary in
Birmingham, England. He collapsed and died after
having sex with a female employee after working hours
in her apartment. Death was attributed to carbon

monoxide fumes from a faulty heater. His widow sought $250,000 in workers' compensation payments for "work-related" injury.

HELD   Workers' compensation benefits granted. The deceased's work assignment in England exposed him to the hazards of such encounters. "It is not reasonable to expect that an employee who is on assignment to a distant land will simply stare at the walls of his hotel room after work."

Administrative Law Judge Ruling

. . . .

Is a coach class passenger who uses the first class toilet a trespasser?

Plaintiff was a coach passenger who was directed by a stewardess to use the first class toilet. While waiting in line, she was accosted by defendant, a first class passenger who berated her as a "disgrace" and a "slut," and told her not to "dirty the first class bathroom," but to get back to where she "belonged." The defendant countersued, claiming that plaintiff had "trespassed" on his right to unobstructed access to the first class lavatory.

HELD   Defendant's countersuit dismissed as frivolous, and costs were imposed against his lawyer for filing a claim based on a "silly" theory.

Vaccaro v. Stephens, U.S. Court of Appeals for Ninth Circuit

. . . .

Is G.I. Joe a "doll"?

Hasbro Industries imports "G.I. Joe action figures" from Hong Kong, where they are manufactured. In 1982, the U.S. Customs Service determined that Hasbro would have to pay the customs duties for items classified as "dolls." Hasbro protested that G.I. Joe should enter under the lower customs duties for "toy figures of animate objects." Thus, the U.S. Court of Appeals for the Federal Circuit confronted a question with grave social consequences: Were all the boys who play with G.I. Joe actually playing with dolls?

HELD   Hasbro supplied a specific biographical sketch for each figure, thus inviting "intimate and manipulative play." The court found that G.I. Joe's unique personalities distinguished him from the "identical, immobile, faceless toy soldiers of yesteryear that were sold in groups of a dozen or so in bags. . . . Even though G.I. Joe has lost this battle, hopefully he will not lose his courage for combat, despite being officially designated by the United States Customs Service as a 'doll.' "

Columnist Gerald Kloss of the *Milwaukee Journal* lamented the decision with a poem which concluded,

> *The moral: Boys like soldier toys*
> *That act real tough and hold long grudges.*

Girls like dolls of curls and poise,
And so, we see, do federal judges.

. . . .

How do you Spell "Relief?"

The plaintiff was an eighth grader who came in second in the county spelling bee. He complained that the contestant who beat him was allowed to advance to the finals even though he spelled "H-O-R-S-Y" as "H-O-R-S-E-Y." Contest officials responded that either spelling is correct, and plaintiff's suit was dismissed. On appeal, Justice Arthur Gilbert of the California Court of Appeal asked, "When should an attorney say 'no' to a client? Answer: When asked to file a lawsuit like this one."

HELD   The suit was properly dismissed. "As the law disregards trifles, one should not trifle with the Court of Appeal. . . . As for the judgment of the trial court, we'll spell it out. A-F-F-I-R-M-E-D." *McDonald v. John P. Scripps Newspaper,* California Court of Appeal.

4

THE JOY OF
EPITHETS

"I would be loathe to speak ill of any person who I do not know deserves it, but I am afraid he is an attorney."
SAMUEL JOHNSON

"That is no slander, sir, which is a truth."
WILLIAM SHAKESPEARE, ROMEO AND JULIET (IV,
i, 33)

"Observe the ass, for instance: his character is about perfect, he is the choicest spirit among all the humbler animals, yet see what ridicule has brought him to. Instead of feeling complimented when we are called an ass, we are left in doubt."
MARK TWAIN, PUDDN'HEAD WILSON

Consider the lamentation of Justice Robert A. Gardner, when confronted with a robbery defendant who had greeted his victim with the salutation, "Don't say a word, don't say a mother-fucking word":

It is sad commentary on contemporary culture to compare "Don't say a word, don't say a mother-fucking word" with "Stand and deliver," the famous salutation of Dick Turpin and other early English highwaymen. It is true that both salutations lead to robbery. However, there is a certain rich style to "Stand and deliver." . . . The speech of contemporary criminal culture has always been a rich source of color and vitality to any language. Yet, when one compares the "bawds," "strumpets," "trulls," "cut-purses," "knaves," and "rascals" of Fielding and Smollett to the "hookers," "pimps," "narcs," "junkies," and "snitches" of today's criminal argot, one wonders just which direction we are traveling civilization's ladder.

．．．．．．．．．．．．．．．．

Prosecutor Arthur N. Bishop collected and annotated all the names prosecutors have applied to criminal defendants. The result is a rather pedestrian assemblage. Only rarely do prosecutors rise to great heights of invective. They have mastered zoology, though, if the catalog of animals they compare the accused to is any indication. Among the names appellate courts have approved for application to criminal defendants are: ape, cattle, cow, crow, dirty dog, mad dog, gorilla, hog, hyena, jackal, leech, yellow rat, rattlesnake, serpent, skunk, vulture, wolf, and worm. Occasionally, prosecutors are inspired to the oratorical splendor achieved by the Missouri district attorney in *State v. Richter,* who suggested the defendant "ought to be shot through the mouth of a red hot cannon, through a barb wire fence into the jaws of hell," but only after he was "kicked in the seat of the pants by a Missouri mule and thrown into a manure pile to rot."

. . . .

In *People v. Williamson,* the defendant complained that the prosecutor called the defense witnesses "egg-sucking, chicken-stealing gutter trash." The court noted that previous California decisions concluded that appropriate epithets for criminal defendants included "a parasite on the community," "a moral leper," "a vile ulcer," and "a moral cancer on the breast of humanity." Apparently, California prosecutors favor allusions to health. Nonetheless, the court suggested that "extravagant and opprobrious" invective should be avoided.

. . . .

LAWYER   What was her response to that information?
WITNESS   She said she would take the child if she couldn't have her visit with him.
LAWYER   Were those her exact words?
WITNESS   Her exact words were she would take the fucking kid.
DEFENDANT   I never said that. You're a fucking liar.

· · · · · · · · · · · · · · · ·

San Francisco lawyer James MacInnis was questioning prospective jurors during his representation of
teamster union officials charged with extortion:

Ladies and gentlemen, and I address myself principally now
to you ladies on the jury. My clients . . . are not nice people.
They're not the kind of people I would want to have in
my house, and certainly not the kind of people you would
have in your home. In fact, they are goons.
  Being rather low class people they speak in rather vulgar
terms and you will, alas, for my side, often hear them using
filthy language. You will hear the defendant refer to the
eminent barrister, Jake Ehrlich, whose presence adorns the
courtroom this morning, as a prick.

The women were shocked, but MacInnis went on.

I see you reel, and understandably so. I must tell you, you
will hear them on one occasion refer to the United States
Attorney, a most distinguished man, and a friend of mine, as
a, forgive me, cocksucker and a fucking little prick.

The ladies were about to faint. The judge intervened
asking if this was serving any purpose. MacInnis replied:

It serves a purpose, Your Honor, or otherwise I wouldn't
be doing it. It serves as the introduction to my next question,
which I address to all of you. Is there anyone on this panel
who, upset as they now are by the kind of language, cannot
make the distinction of being vulgar, being a slob, being

the kind of persons they are, and being guilty of the crime of extortion which they are accused of now? If you cannot do that, say so on your oath now. Serve your country, serve justice . . .

As the case methodically developed, the defendants started to swear. The ladies of the jury were smiling as if thinking to themselves, "I heard all this before; it's nothing." MacInnis won the case.

. . . .

When epithets are applied to police officers, the courts give wide berth to the First Amendment freedom of speech. Consider the opinion of California Court of Appeal Justice Gerald Brown, reviewing the conviction for "uttering offensive words" of a man named Callahan who called a California highway patrolman a "fucking asshole." To avoid continuous repetition of this phrase, "which arguably would assist its passage into parlor parlance," the court referred to it as the "Callahan epithet":

This nation prides itself as unsurpassed in upholding the freedom of its people to express themselves as they see fit without fear, subject only to certain reasonable conditions prescribed by law.

A land as diverse as ours must expect and tolerate an infinite variety of expression. What is vulgar to one may be lyric to another. Some people spew four-letter words as their common speech such as to devalue its currency; their repetition dulls the sense; Billingsgate thus becomes commonplace. Not everyone can be a Daniel Webster, a William Jennings Bryan, or a Joseph A. Ball.

Some writers exalt sex and earthy words to sell their books. Not everyone is a Louis L'Amour, whose hero swears if at all under his breath and whose heroine's suggestiveness, at most, is to walk away, her shoulders prim, her hips less so. . . .

Fifty years ago the words "damn" and "hell" were as shocking to the sensibilities of some people as the Callahan epithet is to others today.* The first word in Callahan's epithet has many meanings. When speaking about coitus, not everyone can be a Frederick E. Smith (later Earl of Birkenhead), who, in his speech in 1920 in the House of Commons on the Matrimonial Causes Act, referred to "that bond by which nature in its ingenious telepathy has contrived to secure and render agreeable the perpetuation of the species."

A farmer, when asked why he struck his mule on the head with a two-by-four, responded, "I am trying to get his attention." Here Dr. Callahan was trying to get the officer's attention to a situation he perceived as requiring medical attention. Under the circumstances here, Callahan's epithet was not inherently likely to provoke an immediate violent reaction.

. . . .

Surprisingly, Justice Brown made no reference to the prior decision of the California Court of Appeal in *In*

---

*Who in that earlier generation can forget the shock wave generated by Clark Gable when as Rhett Butler he said to Scarlett, "Frankly, my dear, I don't give a damn." (Sidney Howard, screenplay for "Gone with the Wind" [1939].) Also, "My dear, I don't give a damn." (Rhett Butler to Scarlet O'Hara in *Gone with the Wind*, Margaret Mitchell [1936].) (John Bartlett, *Familiar Quotations* [15th ed., 1980], p. 848)

Re Price. There, the court upheld a finding that a 17-year-old boy could be convicted of speaking obscene words in public for calling police officers "fucking pigs" and "mother fuckers." Justice Robert Thompson dissented, protesting:

The term "f——g pigs" in the context in which it was used referred not to the copulation of porcine animals but was rather a highly insulting epithet directed to the police officers. . . . Appellant's use of the vulgarism describing the filial partner in an oedipal relationship is fairly to be viewed as an epithet rather than as a phrase appealing to a shameful or morbid interest in intra-family sex. . . . There is, after all, a strong possibility that an expert witness called in the matter before us might have testified to the occasional use of the offending profane adjective in bar association quarters or in trial judges' lounges—alas, all too often in reference to a decision of the Court of Appeal.

. . . .

Not infrequently, lawyers apply epithets to witnesses, each other, or even the judge. Rufus Choate, one of the greatest advocates of the early nineteenth century, we are told by his biographer, "could be as terrible as the Recording Angel, and his tongue had the edge of a Damascus blade" in denouncing witnesses. In an insurance fraud trial, he branded the prosecution's star witness "a vagabond and a villain" who interwove truth with "the scarlet tissue of falsehood." His cutting tongue could be directed toward judges, too. Choate was occasionally heard to describe one judge or another as "an old woman," "a fool," "unable to put two ideas together," or "bigoted as the devil." On one memorable occasion, all of these appellations were applied to the same judge.

Clarence Darrow also dispensed invective liberally. Darrow's denunciation of Harry Orchard, the prime witness in the trial of Bill Haywood for the murder of Idaho Governor Frank Steunenberg, is a classic of the genre:

He is unique in history. If he is not the biggest murderer who ever lived, he is the biggest liar, at least, who ever lived . . . Why, gentlemen, if Harry Orchard were George Washington, who had come into a court of justice with his great name behind him, and if he was impeached and contradicted by as many as Harry Orchard has been, George Washington would go out of it disgraced and counted the Ananias of the age.

The biblical illusion (Ananias lied to St. Peter; see chapter 5, Acts of the Apostles) would not be lost on modern jurors. They still read the Bible occasionally. It's the modern lawyers who don't.

. . . .

Lawyer responding to objection by his opponent during a deposition: "You are an obnoxious little twit. Keep your mouth shut."

The lawyer was fined $250 plus $693 in costs for this outburst.

"Could we hear the part again where the defense calls you a bald-headed, four-eyed, pea-brained old coot?"

. . . .

What happens when the judge himself hurls epithets from the bench? A California municipal court judge, while reprimanding a defendant for coming late in a traffic matter, extended the middle finger of his right hand in a vulgar gesture which the California Supreme Court labeled "digitus impudicus." The judge was removed from office for a variety of other misconduct. With respect to judicial extension of "the finger," however, the court ruled it was not willful misconduct because it "edified the defendant."

. . . .

In *Schleper v. Ford Motor Co.*, the United States Court of Appeals for the Eighth Circuit concluded that one who responded to written interrogatories by writing "Fuck you" could not be held in contempt. Consider this letter which one Arizona lawyer sent to another, with a copy to the judge:

HAND DELIVERED—PERSONAL

Mr. John A. Allison
Allison, McSorley & Kennard
187 W. Main Street
Phoenix AZ 85003

Re: *Foley v. Farmers Ins.*
Cause No. D826593

Dear John:

Evidently you are up to your old tricks again! Knowing that Judge Walters would not cotton to your usual "ex-parte tricks" you have evidently attempted to sway His Honor with this surreptitious, untrue, unkind letter of April 23, 1974.

Regarding you and your comments I have but this to say:

FUCK YOU

Strong letter to follow.

Very truly yours,

Wallace B. Younger

WBY:dm

cc Hon. James A. Walters

. . . .

With some regularity, epithets are the subject of libel and slander litigation. Occasionally, the results are amusing:

. . . The Georgia Supreme Court held that a newspaper editor who was labeled a "turkey" in print by his employer could sue for libel, since the "turkey" label can connote "ineptitude, dumbness, and ignorance."

. . . A Los Angeles woman filed suit against Time, Inc., when her weekly issue of *Time* began arriving with an address label reading:

Mrs. John Smith
5941 Evergreen Terrace
Stupid Ass
Los Angeles, California 90068

. . . A professional football players agent sued the coach of the Denver Gold for calling him a "sleaze-bag" who "slimed up from the bayou." In dismissing the suit, U.S. District Judge Jim Carrington ruled, "It is difficult to imagine how the defendants could prove that the plaintiff is a 'sleaze-bag,' or how the plaintiff could prove that he is not, and therefore the statement is so incapable of factual proof or disproof that it cannot be defamatory in a system of law where truth is a defense."

. . . .

In *King v. Burris,* one baseball franchise owner sued another for a tirade at an owners' meeting which included calling him a "damn fat fag," "fatso," and "liar," and concluding with the question, "Why don't you do the game of baseball a favor and resign?" Judge Kane commented that these comments were "hardly reminiscent of Cyrano de Bergerac's nose speech among baseball's contributions to the art of insult," then catalogued those contributions in a memorable footnote:

See, e.g., "There is no reason why the field should not try to put the batsman off his stroke at the critical moment by neatly timed disparagements of his wife's fidelity and his mother's respectability."
George Bernard Shaw

"[H]is head was full of larceny, but his feet were honest."
"Bugs" Bear on outfielder Ping Bodie, 1917

"Call me anything, Call me m——— f——— but don't call me Durocher. A Durocher is the lowest form of living matter."
Harry Wendelstedt, 1974

"The more we lose, the more Steinbrenner will fly in. And the more he flies, the better chance there will be a plane crash."
Craig Nettles, 1977

"(Charley Finley) would want to know why there were fourteen uniforms dirty when only ten men got in the game."
Frank Ciensczk, Oakland equipment manager, 1972

"I have often called Bowie Kuhn a village idiot. I apologize to all the village idiots of America. He is the nation's idiot."
Charlie Finley, 1981

"The best way to test a Timex would be to strap it to [Earl] Weaver's tongue."
Marty Springstead, umpire

"As a lifetime Cubs fan, I was used to players who, as the sportswriters say, 'can do it all.' In the case of the Cubs, 'doing it all' means striking out, running the wrong way, falling down, dropping the ball."
Mike Royko, writer

. . . .

Just as troublesome to the courts has been the more frequent appellation "son of a bitch." In an erudite study, Saul Cohen collected all the cases in which courts have considered the etymology and embellishment of this old favorite. Some highlights:

. . . In *Louisville & N.R. Co. v. Lindsay,* the plaintiff sued a railroad because of the words used by an employee. The yard clerk said to him that anybody who said that he had stolen a dog was a "God damn lying son of a bitch." The court held that the railroad was not liable as the employee was engaged in a personal matter.

. . . An argument over the weight of a chicken was the catalyst in *Huckabee v. Nash.* Each testified that the other had called him a "God damned s—— of a b——." In view of the mutual exchange of opprobrious epithets, no recovery was allowed. The trial court gave the following instruction, held to be correct:

The court instructs the jury for the defendant that even though you may believe from the evidence that defendant,

Dr. N. L. Nash, called plaintiff, William Huckabee, a son of a bitch, yet if you further believe from the evidence that immediately before this, the said Huckabee had called Dr. Nash a son of a bitch, and that Dr. Nash called Huckabee a son of bitch on the impulse of the moment and in the heat of passion, and in retaliation for what Huckabee had called him, then you will find your verdict for the defendant. . . .

. . . In *Southeastern Greyhound Corp. v. Graham,* the defendant's bus driver, one Turnipseed, in the aftermath of an altercation about the closing of a window, "turned towards petitioner and loudly exclaimed, to wit: 'You God-damned bald-headed son of a bitch, step over here and I'll settle the whole damn business with you.' "

. . . In *Gilardino v. Patorno,* it appears likely that either the plaintiff (a female) or the defendant (a male) or each of them called the other a son of a bitch, but the court does not quote the actual language used during the course of the running argument. The court refers to the words and phrases used as "a very ugly epithet," "another epithet, uglier, if possible, than the first," "a very bad name, indeed," "two about as ugly epithets as the soft and beautiful Italian language affords," "epithets which are entirely taboo in polite society," and "epithet reflecting not only on defendant's personal character, but upon his ancestors, as well."

There is a report, probably apocryphal, of another southern trial, involving a plaintiff who had been called "a lying thieving son of a bitch." The defense was truth, and with respect to the first two accusations the defense showed that the plaintiff had been a persistent liar since childhood and that he had twice been convicted of larceny. As its final witness, the defense called a tall, lean, sun-tanned gentleman who, in answer to the question, "What is your business or profession?" stated that he was "a judge of sons o' bitches." In stating his qualifications, the witness said, "Out in Texas we got a lot of 'em and my business is knowing how to spot 'em. I can spot one a mile away on a clear day." He was asked to look carefully at the plaintiff and give his expert opinion. He looked, turned to the jury and said, "Gentlemen, he's a son of a bitch if I ever saw one!"

. . . .

Bankruptcy Judge Stanley B. Bernstein expressed the frustration of bankruptcy judges everywhere who are called upon to determine "reasonable attorney's fees" in bankruptcy cases. He found an outlet for his frustration in *The Joys of Yiddish:*

The primary units of the ordinal scale are as follows: (1) *Maeven*   A "maeven" deserves a premium of at least 20% over his normal hourly rate. He is the "expert's expert." The Eighth Circuit in *Ramos v. Lamm,* 713 F.2d 546 (10th Cir. 1983), has already recognized the "genius factor" in fee petitions; (2) *Noch Schlepper*   A "noch schlepper" deserves a 20% discount from his normal hourly rate. He "drags along" to hearings and meetings, offering little insight and occupying an extra chair. This characteristic is sometimes institutionalized in the role of the attorney for the creditors' committee or co-counsel for the debtor; (3) *Koch Leffle*   A "koch leffle" deserves a 30% discount from his normal hourly rate. He keeps "stirring the pot" by raising frivolous objections to claims, by moving for reconsideration, or by rearguing points thoroughly canvassed in earlier weeks of the case; (4) *Yolt* A "yolt" deserves at least a 50% discount from his normally hourly rate. He is the "boisterous fool" who is always objecting to the form of the question, arguing the "best evidence rule," threatening appeals from routine interlocutory orders, objecting to the interest rate charged to corporations as usurious, and repeatedly moving for adjournment on the day of the hearing whenever out-of-town counsel attend; (5) *Gahniff* A "gahniff" deserves at least a 75% discount from his normal hourly rate, if not suspension from the bar. He is the classic "thief" who runs a Chapter 7 mill—he plans fraudulent transfer for his clients. He performs all of his services through poorly supervised paralegals and rotating associates, he deliberately understates his retainer on his Rule 2016 affidavit, and he fails to appear at pretrials on nondischargeability complaints because his boilerplate fee agreement is limited to filing the petition, schedules, and attending the meeting of creditors. At the Section 341 meeting, he either cannot recognize his client or advises him to plead the Fifth Amendment.

· · · · · · · · · · · · · · · ·

5

BEASTS BEFORE
THE BAR

*"Allow not nature more than nature needs,
Man's life's as cheap as beast's."*
    WILLIAM SHAKESPEARE, KING LEAR (II, iv, 267)

"Every dog is entitled to one bite."

                                      PROVERB

*"If an object looks like a duck, walks like a duck and quacks like
a duck, it is likely to be a duck."*
    JUSTICE STANLEY MOSK, IN RE DEBORAH C.

A heated patent infringement trial was underway in federal court, Duluth, Minnesota. Plaintiff claimed defendant appropriated his design for a beaver trap. Defendant claimed that plaintiff's trap was designed to trap larger animals, not beavers.

Plaintiff called a retired professor of zoology, who began the morning session with extensive discourse on beaver habits. During the noon recess, defense counsel had one martini too many, returning to court belligerent to begin his cross-examination:

Q. What do zoologists do, Professor?

A. They study and sometimes teach animal life. There are many varied branches and specialities. I know a professor who spent thirty-five years studying the snail family.

Q. Where is he now?

THE COURT What has that got to do with this matter? You are wandering far afield.

COUNSEL Your Honor forgets this is cross-examination.

THE COURT I don't forget anything of the kind. Get along with your questions.

COUNSEL Strike it. We will start all over again. I will try to put my questions in such a simple childlike way that even a dignified, educated professor who comes from the north woods telling us, as if we didn't know, what beavers do—

OPPOSING COUNSEL I certainly want to object to these remarks.

THE COURT Yes, that is very objectionable. Ask your questions. You aren't testifying. Get down to the meat of the thing.

Counsel   Very well, Your Honor. The sneering,
contemptuous, supercilious attitude of this
witness toward me has so outraged me
that perhaps I have lost my temper.

Q.   So you say you are a specialist on beavers
and snails?

A.   I didn't say any such thing. I said I know
a great deal about beavers and many
animals. I have lived with them. I have
observed and handled them. They have a
sort of language, you know. The cruelest
thing we can call them is dumb animals
and—

Q.   You say they can talk?

A.   Well, there is a sense in which all nature
has a language which we—

Q.   Answer my question. You said a beaver
can talk.

A.   All animals can speak. They communicate
with one another and understand their
own language. Even—

Q.   Can you speak it?

A.   Yes.

Counsel   I want the reporter to get this. This is
good. Mr. Reporter, be sure and get this.

The court   He is getting it.

Witness   I was about to say that even plant life has
a kind of language.

Q.   Do you talk that too? Answer yes or no.

A.   Subject to what I have said, I will answer
yes.

Q.   Did you ever talk to a buttercup?

A.   Well, to those who are familiar with them and love them, some flowers have a certain language.

Q.   What did the buttercup say to you and what did you say to the buttercup, fixing the time and place as well as you can?

THE COURT   You don't have to answer such a question.

Q.   Did you ever talk to a giraffe?

A.   I can't answer yes or no. I think I can in a sense speak their language, making them understand me, my motives, wishes, and so on.

Q.   Then you have talked to a giraffe?

A.   Yes, with that qualification.

Q.   And the giraffe talked to you?

A.   Yes.

Q.   Did you ever talk to a lion?

A.   Yes.

Q.   Did you ever talk to a skunk?

A.   Yes.

Q.   And it talked to you?

A.   Yes.

Q.   Well the next time you talk with one of those bastards, ask him what the hell the big idea is. No further questions.

. . . .

Augusta, Georgia, officials wanted Blackie the Talking Cat to have a business license. Local Augustans had seen Blackie and her owner-agent performing for donations in the business district. Blackie would talk on command while stroked, saying "I love you" and "I want my mama." Blackie also made local TV and radio appearances. The judge agreed to the city demand, noting:

For hundreds, perhaps thousands, of years, people have carried on conversations with cats. Most often, these are one-sided and range from cloying, mawkish nonsense to topics of science and the liberal arts. Apparently Blackie's pride does not prevent him from making an occasional response to this great gush of human verbiage . . . (S)ome cats do talk. Others just grin.

Miles v. City of Atlanta

. . . .

A judicial opinion saving a dog from the "death penalty":

We resist the temptation that grabbed hold of our colleagues who have written dog opinions, and will not try to dig up appropriate sobriquets. You will not read about "unmuzzled liberty." Nor will you consider an argument "dogmatically asserted" or cringe with "we con-cur." We will not subject you to phrases such as "barking up the wrong tree." We disavow doggerel.

Phillips v. Dept. of Animal Regulation

. . . .

A dog owner in Missouri sued under his homeowner's insurance policy for some 75 to 80 spots left by his poodle, André, on the new carpeting. Coverage was claimed under the "floater" provisions, designed to extend to damage based on "fortuitious circumstances other than fire, wind, and rain." In *Aetna Insurance v. Sachs*, the federal district court denied the claim:

In the law, "fortuitous" means "by chance" and "by accident." It seems to me that it is just "by accident" that André didn't do what he did, much before the alleged occurrence, and, if "by chance" he didn't, it was just too much and too often, to require plaintiff to pay for it.

While the suit was pending, André met his demise in a confrontation with a large truck. The court concluded:

[I] am saying to the insured, "You cannot recover"; to the insurer, "You may continue your policy in peace"; and to the beloved little French poodle, the proximate cause of this litigation and discourse, I say, "Paix à toi aussi, André."

(Translation: Peace to you also, André.)

. . . .

Larry Freukes was charged with shooting his wife's lover. His defense was that the gun accidentally discharged when his large poodle caught its paw in the trigger and knocked the gun to the floor. Freukes's version of the incident wasn't helped by testimony that he had told the victim after the shooting, "I'm in a lot of trouble. You've got to tell them the dog did it." Freukes's conviction was affirmed on appeal.

"And you expect this Court to believe that my client broke a chair belonging to you, a 1200-pound bear, by sitting on it?"

. . . .

The revered old common law punished grand larceny with death. Thus, courts ruled one could not
"steal" a dog or cat because, as Lord Cooke wrote, "[I]t
was not fit that a person should die for a dog." It was
larceny to steal a tame hawk but not a tame dog, unless
the dog was dead and the thief took only its hide!

. . . .

A wrongful-death action for Peter the Great, a canine celebrity of the late 1920s, evoked a passionate
plea in the brief from plaintiff's counsel:

[I]t must be remembered that Peter the Great was a motion
picture star, he was a gift to humanity. Peter the Great
is a name that will go down in history as the most human
dog that ever displayed its skill in a film drama. His name
was a symbol of loyalty, devotion, nobility, and heroic ex-
ploits. He made the multitude laugh and cry, wonder and
admire. Peter the Great sent them to their homes with pictures of high ideals and unselfish service; the clean and pure,
the good in thought, example, and action. Peter the Great
was a by-word of every household, a wonder-word to every
child lover of the motion picture world. And when he came
to the last scene, in the drama of life, when the curtain
of death was slowly ringing down and he was going into
that long, long sleep . . . he seemed to smile as the lights
went out.

Dreyer v. Cyriacks

. . . .

In 1983, the Montana Supreme Court upheld the award of $240,000 in damages to a Beaverhead County farmer because the state's nearby highway construction was stressful to his pigs. The landmark case of *Howery v. Montana* included expert testimony by Missoula veterinarian Earl Pruyn about "porcine stress syndrome."

. . . .

A police officer in Baltimore stopped a man who was walking oddly down a street with enormous bulges in his pants. After he was stopped, the suspect began shaking and pulling pigeons from inside his pants. In all, he pulled out 21 live pigeons and five dead ones. He was charged with stealing the homing pigeons from a neighbor, and cruelty to animals. "He looked like the Michelin tire ad," reported the arresting officer.

. . . .

In the quiet California community of Bishop, a judge issued this order describing how certain community property would be divided in a marital dissolution case:

3. Custody of the dog—This issue will be decided in accordance with: A) What is for the dog's best interest. The issue of custody of the dog will be referred to the Animal Control Officer for investigation and report. B) The age of the dog

is sufficient to indicate that the desire of the dog regarding custody should be given consideration.

. . . .

A New York Supreme Court justice ordered a "behavioral and mental examination" of a dog in *People v. Goodfriend.* The defendant was charged with assault but claimed that the crime was not possible because the victim owned a large and vicious German shepherd. Not so, claimed the prosecutor, the canine is a mixed breed with a "meek disposition" and "quite docile." To resolve the dispute, Fido was off to the Animal Behavior Therapy Clinic for a complete psychological workup and determination whether it "exhibits any aggressive behavior in response to certain stimuli."

. . . .

Cross-examination during an insanity trial in federal court:

    Q. You will agree with me, Doctor, that the manner in which you get information from someone sitting for a diagnosis is by asking about family background?

    A. Only partly. A small part.

    Q. Do you believe you could diagnose an animal, a dog, as having psychoneurosis?

    A. I think I could. I have owned several dogs.

    Q. Do you talk to animals, Doctor?

    A. Yes.

COUNSEL No further questions.

PROSECUTOR   I have no questions. Request the doctor be
               excused to return to the hospital, Your
               Honor.
COUNSEL   If he can find his way back, I have no
               objection.
WITNESS   If I can't, I will ask a dog on the corner.

· · · · · · · · · · · · · · ·

Young Larry O'Dowd of York, England, was fined
for using abusive language and behavior likely to breach
the peace. A local officer had ordered the teen and
some friends to disperse from a street corner. As he
departed, O'Dowd turned and said "Meow" to the
cop's German shepherd. The officer found that provoc-
ative and a scuffle ensued. An enraged local member of
Parliament said he was going to protest the sentence to
the head of the British judiciary.

· · · · · · · · · · · · · · ·

And, with dogs' being our best friend, who can fault
inmate Winfield Hanson for wanting to have visits
from "Puji" while he was serving time for 33 felony
counts? Tucson, Arizona, Judge Lillian Fisher agreed
to consider the request, especially when Hanson indicated that his wife would be willing to accompany Puji
and that Puji's life expectancy is shorter than Hanson's
prison term.

· · · · · · · · · · · · · · ·

Where's Dumbo? Some years ago, the federal court
in Los Angeles was the scene of a vicious custody battle

over an elephant. Who could forget it? Paul and Judy Kaye's marriage went sour and Judy wanted Dumbo, who used to belong to Judy's mother but had ended up with Paul, who is a circus producer. Got all that? Well, Dollie—Judy's mother—sued Paul because she wanted to know where Dumbo was and he kept the pachyderm hidden from her, threatening to mistreat or sell Dumbo if Dollie refused to sign a contract of sale. But then Dollie died. So Judy entered the fracas, saying that Dumbo was her "sister" because they were raised together. The case ended up in federal court because the litigants lived in different states. Last word was that Dumbo was gainfully employed somewhere in South Dakota. Extradition was considered unlikely.

. . . .

In Danbury, Connecticut, Barbara Nelson pointed the accusatory finger of fatherhood directly at "Tony" for impregnating her "Frosty" and demanded recompense for a canine abortion. The judge scratched his ear and awarded $119 to Nelson, leaving Tony's owner doggone mad and proclaiming, "There was no biological proof of responsibility here. We would have been willing to have Tony submit to a blood test. And don't we have rights as grandparents?"

"Max" of Shaker Heights, Ohio, made off better. All paternity charges involving some 16 puppies were dismissed in small claims court. The surrogate plaintiff claimed that he saw a male dog attempting to mate with his canine and, when chased, running to the defendant's garage. Sixty-two days later, he unwillingly grandfathered a litter. The judge ruled that the proof was insufficient and there were no reports of Max's having "a reputation for loose behavior."

. . . .

A Washington, D.C., doctor was charged with goose-killing after applying one or more of his golf clubs to a goose sharing the golf course with him. Witnesses said the doc took out after the goose when it continued honking during an important putt. The defendant claimed that the bludgeoning was an act of mercy after an errant slice shot on a par 4 hole put the bird in great misery. A secret plea bargain with the U.S. Attorney kept the final details from the public.

. . . .

The defendant was charged with the crime of vehicular hit-and-run after hitting a dog with his car. The appellate court reviewed the pertinent law requiring that drivers stop after accidents, render aid, and show their driver's license to the person struck. Justice Shaw wrote:

Manifestly, a dog or other animal is not a person; consequently the provision concerning rendering aid cannot be applied . . . Dogs and other animals are not found driving vehicles on the highways, so we hardly think the legislature meant to include them in the term "driver of any vehicle"; and in view of the utter futility of submitting a written document to the inspection of a dog or other animal the term "occupant" must also be limited to persons. It may be that "every dog has his day"; but if so, it is only a "dog day" and does not entitle him to claim the rights of persons.

People v. Fimbres

. . . .

London was the scene of a shocking abuse story. One Eleanor Donoghy, a 16-year-old employee of a fish processing plant, faced charges for cruelty to prawns. She was alleged to have fried them to death instead of boiling them. Some of her colleagues reported her to the Royal Society for the Prevention of Cruelty to Animals after seeing her dump the prawns on a hot stove. She denied the act. Meanwhile, the court and some experts were tangled in appropriate legal questions such as, "What is cruelty?" and whether prawns come within the meaning of the 1912 Protection of Animals Act.

. . . .

Judge Bill Ragan of Houston presided at a cruelty-to-chicken case. The defendant was alleged to have used the chicken as "bait" to train a bulldog; he claimed he was exercising the dog by putting the chicken at the opposite end of a harness and letting the pup try to catch it. Ragan dismissed the case, ruling that he could not determine the chicken's state of mind and it had not been physically abused because it missed not a single feather. In rare form, the tribunal ruled:

"Relax. This is court-ordered so it's pro bono."

There was no testimony about whether the chicken was afraid, frightened, cackling, flapping its wings or enjoying its ride on this merry-go-round. [T]he chicken [may have] enjoyed riding on a merry-go-round like our children enjoy. Lord, it's difficult enough to decide cases with human beings, much less a chicken.

. . . .

Velna Turnage sued Christy Brothers Circus for $500 in damages for mental suffering, humiliation, and embarrassment arising out of her attendance at the defendant's circus. In the Georgia court's own words:

[W]hile [the plaintiff was] in attendance as a guest of the defendant at a circus performance and while seated in one of the seats provided by the defendant, a horse, which was going through a dancing performance immediately in front of where the plaintiff was sitting, was by the defendant's servant, who was riding upon the horse, caused to back towards the plaintiff, and while in this situation the horse evacuated his bowels into her lap . . . in full view of many people . . . all of whom laughed at the occurrence . . .

. . . .

When confronted with the case of *Selmon v. Hasbro Bradley, Inc.,* in which plaintiffs claimed the defendants swiped their copyrighted idea of marketing stuffed animals combining the characteristics of two animals, U.S. District Judge Goettel of White Plains, New York, just couldn't resist:

Once upon a time, in lands far, far away, lived strange but cuddly creatures that became involved in a struggle for identity. In "Whatland," which is just a few miles north of Fairyland, lived the "Whats." In the "Land of Wuz" lived the "Wuzzles." We don't know where "Wuz" was, but we are told we could get there if we "snuzzle a Wuzzle." It appears that for a time, never the two did meet. But one day the creators of the "Whats" discovered the "Wuzzles" and were astonished to learn that "Whats" and "Wuzzles" had certain similarities. Most specifically, it seems each "What" and "Wuzzle" had the names and characteristics of two different animals combined into one. In "Whatland," there was "Me-ouse" (a mouse and cat combined), "Wissh" (a walrus and seal), "Chuck" (a chicken and duck), "Skeet" (a skunk and parakeet), "Pea-tur" (a peacock and turkey), "Gir-itch" (a giraffe and ostrich), "Leo-Lamo" (a lion and lamb), and "Beav-aire" (a beaver and bear). The "Wuzzles" included "Moosel" (a moose and seal), "Butterbear" (a butterfly and bear), "Hoppopotamus" (a rabbit and hippopotamus), "Eleroo" (an elephant and kangaroo), "Rhinokey" (a rhinoceros and monkey), and "Bumbelion" (a bumblebee and lion).

Our story now moves to its sad conclusion. The creators of the "Whats," who were protected by copyright, were outraged and thought that the creators of the "Wuzzles" had stolen their idea. A lawsuit broke out, with the plaintiffs, creators of the "What," alleging violation of the federal copyright laws and unjust enrichment. The defendants, creators of the "Wuzzles," have moved for summary judgment, as well as attorney's fees and sanctions under 17 U.S.C. Sec. 505 of the Copyright Act, 28 U.S.C. Sec. 1927, and rule 11 of the Federal Rules of Civil Procedure for plaintiffs' pursuit of allegedly frivolous and vexatious litigation.

This battle on high between creators has filtered down to

us in this "What"-less and "Wuzzle"-less Land of White Plains. The questions before us are really quite simple: "Just what's a 'What,' what's the similarity between a 'What' and a 'Wuzzle,' and 'Wuzzle' we do about it?"

. . . .

6

THE NAMES IN
THE GAME

"What's in a name? That which we call a rose
By any other name would smell as sweet."
WILLIAM SHAKESPEARE, ROMEO AND JULIET (II, ii, 43)

PROSECUTOR	Who's insane?
DEFENDANT	Who is he?
PROSECUTOR	I mean—is there somebody in the gang called Insane?
DEFENDANT	Yeah.
PROSECUTOR	Is there a Big Insane?
DEFENDANT	Yeah.
PROSECUTOR	Is there a Little Insane?
DEFENDANT	Yeah.
PROSECUTOR	You don't happen to know their Christian names by any chance, do you?
DEFENDANT	Their Christian names?
PROSECUTOR	Yeah, like Bill, Charlie, you know, Fred?
DEFENDANT	Perfectly honest, I never knew they was Christian.

. . . .

Unlikely-but-True Case Names

Sand v. Beach, 200 N.E. 821 (N.Y. 1936)

Plough v. Fields, 422 F. 2d 824 (9th Cir. 1970)

In re Worms, 252 Cal. App. 2d 130 (1967)

People v. Slutts, 259 Cal. 2d 886 (1968)

People v. Bimbo, 145 N.E. 651 (1924)

People v. Takencareof, 174 Cal. Rptr. 112 (1981)

State v. Gopher, 633 P. 2d 1195 (Montana 1981)

People v. Ah Own, Ah Sing, Ah You and Ah Gum, 39 Cal. 604 (1870)

People v. Justice, 167 Cal. App. 2d 616 (1959)

Coffin v. Bloodworth, 28 Cal. App. 2d 522 (1938)

Pain v. Municipal Court, 237 Cal. App. 2d 151 (1968)

Anger v. Municipal Court, 237 Cal. App. 2d 69
(1965)
*Easter Seal Society for Crippled Children v. Playboy
Enterprises* (6th Cir. 1987) 815 F. 2d 323
King v. The Queen, 1 A.C. 304 (1969)
Silver v. Gold, 259 Cal. Rptr. 185 (1989)
McSomebodies, et al. v. *San Mateo City School
District,* 89 C.D.O.S. 7473 (U.S. Dist. Ct., N.D.
Calif., 1989)

. . . .

Defendants arrested in California frequently give
phony names. If the arresting officers are unable to
immediately ascertain the true name of the defendant,
they simply book them under the name supplied. That
explains how George Washington, Thomas Jefferson,
Abraham Lincoln, and nearly every other president
have shown up on the docket of the criminal arraign-
ment court in Los Angeles. Other recent filings have
included Pretty Boy Floyd, Mae West, Levi Strauss
and Jesus Christ. One forgery case was filed under the
name the suspect used to sign a check: Youra Sucker.

. . . .

The public defender for Broward County, Florida,
had an unusual set of client names all within a short
span. He was appointed to represent a defendant by the
name of Earl Outlaw, charged with armed robbery.
Next he got a juvenile on a theft charge. His name?

. . . Robin Hood. But it wasn't long before he was assigned another alleged shoplifter—this one named Claude Crook, who was being prosecuted by State Attorney Janice Law!

. . . .

Law firm names:

> Ketcham & Cheatem (Georgia)
> Wild & Wooley (California)
> Gooing & Cumming (California)
> Silver & Gold (New York)

And then there was the San Jose attorney named Stromer, whose client's name was Banjo.

. . . .

Prisoners frequently come up with nicknames for the judges who sentenced them. Every courthouse, it seems, has a "Maximum (fill-in-the-blank)." Washington, D.C., Judge John Sirica of Watergate fame was known as "Maximum John." Around the federal courthouse in Los Angeles, "Maximum" was passed from one generation of judge to the next, from "Maximum Mathes" in the 1950s (U.S. District Judge William Mathes) to "Maximum Malcolm" in the '70s (now Chief Justice Malcolm Lucas of the California Supreme Court). Judge Mathes earned the sobriquet by commencing every sentencing asking the defendant's lawyer, "Is there any reason the maximum sentence should not be imposed in this case?"

Inmates in New York have a more creative bent. They have renamed the city prison on Rikers Island as "Galligan's Island," in honor of Justice Thomas B. Gallagan who probably sent more of them there for longer stays than any other judge in New York City. Another New York judge, Justice Edwin Torres, is known as the "time machine." Before sentencing one murderer to a 57-year term, Justice Torres said, "His parole officer hasn't been born yet."

. . . .

Customized "named" license plates can be clever— unless carried too far. In *Katz v. Department of Motor Vehicles* plaintiff requested an order that DMV issue him plates reading "EZ LAY." DMV denied the request on grounds that the requested combination of letters was offensive. Katz countered that the DMV had issued 26 other plates which were just as offensive, producing the following list: BALL, BALLS, BFD, BIPPY, BJ, BOOBS, BS, DIK, EAT OUT, EZ HOOK, FCK, FERN, FUCHS, HOOKER, HOT BOD, HOT BOX, HORNEE, HORNY, KILLER, PUSSY, 4 PLAY, SCREW 2, SLEEZ, SLEEZY, STUD, VIRGIN. The court held that 26 slip-ups out of 102,000 personalized plates wasn't bad, and that was no reason to make it 27. Thus, you won't find an "EZ LAY" on the freeways of California.

. . . .

Another Californian won the right to list his last name, "Schmuck," on his personalized plate, despite its inclusion on the DMV "list" of offensive or insulting names. He claimed that he did not intend that anyone translate his name into the Yiddish name for penis and would sue to uphold the meaning of his proper German name: "jewel." Fortunately, he omitted his first name from the plates—Peter.

. . . .

Some people use the law to change their names . . . and others probably should! A sample of some name change filings:

Present name: Chung Hua Asavavallop
Proposed name: Austin Asavavallop
Reason for change: Easier to pronounce

Present name: Jung-Hee Ho
Proposed name: Jung-Hee Ro
Reason for change: Suffer inconvenience

Present name: Hwa Cha Mullady
Proposed name: Hee Won Chi
Reason for change: Wants to use maiden name but cannot use it with "Hwa Cha" because that name is associated with a Korean bar hostess who caters to pleasures of men.

Present name: Gerardo Herminio Sturdivant
Proposed name: Yerlin Gerard Sturdivant
Reason for change: To comply with family desires and to obtain popularity in business.

Present name: Meredith Roy Saunders
Proposed name: Mazdera Madde Dogge
Reason for change: Petitioner is a "junior" and would like

"Mr. Piggy-Wig can call honorable counsel anything he chooses—Mr. Piggy-Wig is a friend of the Court."

to establish his own identity as an adult and has devised this name, part American Indian, part Islamic, as appropriate for him.

. . . .

A city councilman running for mayor of Garden Grove, California, sought to legally change his name from "Robert Dinsen" to "Robert Frank Taxfighter Bob Dinsen." The request was an attempt to evade a local ordinance prohibiting candidates from using "Taxfighter" as a ballot designation. Three candidates were all calling themselves "taxfighters" or something similar. The request was opposed by a 17-year-old boy, who argued, "Politicians can lie all they want, but they can't subvert the ballot box." The name change was denied.

. . . .

Among ballot designations which California candidates have requested are Mother Trucker, Air Balancer, Journeyman Tinsmith, Outdoor Showman, Philosopher, Shaman, Echo Evangelist, Environmentalist Surfer Artist, and Nun of the Above.

. . . .

Morris Edward Reed wanted his name to be Sunshine Morris Edward Reed, but his request was denied by the trial court. Sunshine appealed to the Missouri Court of Appeals, which ruled for him, noting that he had adopted the sobriquet many years prior "because of his spirit of jocundity, refulgent personality coruscating on those with whom he associated and by reason of his sanguinary outlook on life."

. . . .

A Mineola, New York, attorney happened to like his name but didn't like what was happening to it on a local radio station. He sued for $1.2 million because of a "humiliating" radio commercial placed by a Long Island bank.

The commercial features a man who gets jealous of his neighbor—Solowicz—who buys a swimming pool and expensive stereo. So he gets a bank loan and takes his family on vacation to Hawaii. At the close of the spot, the man remarks, "Lemme tell you, the best part of the trip will be saying, 'Aloha, Solowicz.' "

Lawyer Jack Solerwitz found the commercial uninspiring—in fact, downright "degrading and humiliating." "All I hear," remarked Jack, "is 'Aloha, Solowicz,' " from colleagues and clients. Last word was that the counselor succeeded in getting a temporary restraining order by alleging that because the two names sound the same, the bank was illegally using his name and making him the butt of "taunts and contempt."

. . . .

In 1976, Michael Herbert Dengler petitioned the courts of North Dakota to permit him to change his name to "1069." He explained his unusual request with the thought that a person's name should reflect his personal philosophy. Each digit of his new name would reflect a fact of his philosophy:

The first character, 1, stands for my concept of nature which manifests itself as one individual among the various forms of life. I stand as a single entity amongst millions of other entities, animate and inanimate. But yet even though I am an entity unto myself, I am part of the whole of life which is one. I am one; life is one; and together we are one.

The second character, 0, shows my relationship with time in movement through life; I feel that I recognize a past, experience a present, and am aware of a future with equal regard. I am therefore zero with respect to my march on the road of life.

The third character, 6, is equal to the relationship I have with the universe in my understanding of space or my spatial occupancy through this life.

The fourth and final character, 9, stands for the relationship I have to essence in the difference in the meaning when actualizing the spatially ever-present nature of life. This final digit is like a string which surrounds the entirety of the previous three digits and explains the first three digits' concepts as they interact among each other to produce my philosophy.

The Supreme Court of North Dakota denied his request, noting that use of numbers as names would create widespread confusion. Moreover, no one would know how to pronounce his name: would it be "one thousand sixty-nine," "one naught six nine," "one zero six nine," or would it be "ten sixty nine?"

Dengler then moved to Minnesota, where he proceeded to pass himself off as 1069 anyway. The name was recognized by his bank, the Social Security Administration, and various state agencies. However, the Minnesota Gas Company and the Drivers License Division of the Department of Public Safety refused to recognize the name without a court order. So Dengler petitioned the courts, and worked his way up to the Supreme Court of Minnesota. They denied his petition, but recognized his "common-law right" to call himself whatever he pleased. The court also suggested that he might apply again, using verbal substitutes for the numbers, such as "Ten Sixty Nine" or "One Zero Six Nine." A helpful footnote offered the observation that "the use of a Christian name such as 'One' and surname 'Nine' would not phonetically be unlike the name 'Juan Nyen,' which are somewhat unusual but perfectly acceptable names."

Mr. Dengler reappeared six years later when he applied for a marriage license as 1069. When the application was refused, he petitioned to have his name changed to "Michael 10 Holtz." Even this was denied. But when the judgment was sent by registered mail to Dengler's home, it was returned to the sender with the notation that no Michael Dengler lived at that address. Dengler finally gave in, subtracting the numbers from his name to achieve wedded bliss.

. . . .

A California appellate court agreed that a number is not a name when it told Thomas Boyd Ritchie III that he could not legally change his last name to "III" (pronounced "three"). The court cited the *Dengler* case as precedent, concluding that Ritchie had common law rights to call himself whatever he wanted, but "[T]o call himself a number, even Roman, does not a new 'name' make. Historically and chronologically it may 1984 be, but novelistically we do not with Orwell such foresee."

. . . .

American jurisprudence lets just about anyone sue just about anybody, subject, of course, to some practical limitations—like finding the defendant and serving papers on him. Two actions in particular—actually filed—present a few difficulties for the plaintiff:

United States ex rel. Gerald Mayo v. Satan & His Staff

Alleging numerous occasions where defendant caused plaintiff misery and unwarranted threats, placed deliberate obstacles in his path, and caused his downfall, Mayo sought permission from the federal district court in Pennsylvania to sue Satan for a civil rights violation.

The court denied same, questioning whether Mayo could get personal jurisdiction over the defendant and expressing concern that the next step would be to make this suit a class action, with numerous members making joinder impracticable.

Forbes, All Christian Children, Their Parents, Taxpayers of Arkansas, and *Jesus Christ, Lord,*

*Saviour, Best Friend, Master, King of Kings &
Rightful Sovereign*

vs.

*Department of Education, School District, School
Board, High Priests of Secular Humanism, Communist
Party USA, Church of Satan, The Anti-Christs,* and
Satan, the God of this World System

A Little Rock lawyer decided to file a class action suit in federal court on the day before Halloween, seeking to enjoin the public schools from observing or commemorating the "rites and customs and practices of the religion of Satan on its annual high unholy day." It was not clear how the named defendants joined together, although the complaint made reference to the Mayflower Compact, Columbus, and the charter granted Sir Walter Raleigh.

To everyone's surprise, defendant Satan filed a motion to dismiss the suit. Lawyer John Wesley Hall of Little Rock stepped in as "Devil's Advocate." The motion asserted that the controversy contained in the complaint was between Jesus Christ and Satan and "nonjusticiable" because of the First Amendment; further, that Satan lacked sufficient "minimum contacts" with the state of Arkansas to permit suit in a federal court: plaintiffs did not allege that Satan transacts business, owns property, writes contracts, or commits torts in Arkansas.

. . . .

7

STARE DECISIS

"Our principal task in this case is to determine what the New York courts would think the California courts would think on an issue about which neither has thought."
JUDGE HENRY J. FRIENDLY, NOLAN V.
TRANSOCEAN AIRLINES

" 'Twill be recorded for a precedent,
And many an error by the same example
Will rush into the state."
WILLIAM SHAKESPEARE, MERCHANT OF VENICE
(IV, i, 220)

The doctrine of "stare decisis" normally requires a court to follow its previous decisions, known as "precedents." Much of the research in which lawyers engage is an effort to find precedents which closely resemble their client's case. If the precedent is favorable, the lawyer will urge the court to follow it. If it is unfavorable, the lawyer will suggest it is "distinguishable" because the facts are different, or argue it should be overruled.

. . . .

In the 1965 case of *Birdsell v. United States*, the court rejected an unusual claim of insanity. The defendant sought acquittal on a theft charge on the grounds of a delusion that he was the reincarnation of Confederate General Nathan Bedford Forrest, the first Imperial Wizard of the Ku Klux Klan, and had been specially instructed to forage "for the cause." Twenty years later, the court found this precedent useful when it was again confronted with a claim of insanity based on the defendant's delusion he was the reincarnation of General Nathan Bedford Forrest. The claim was being asserted by the same defendant!

. . . .

A "precedent" which starts a long progression of similar rulings is frequently referred to as the "seminal" case. California Justice Robert Thompson, in *Medovoi v. American Savings*, departed from this timeworn usage to say, "As I analyze the ovular[1] case of *Coast Bank* . . ." He explained in a footnote:

[1]The feminists among us are entitled to a word other than "seminal."

. . . .

On occasion, the judges who must follow precedents of the U.S. Supreme Court have been reluctant to do so. The undisputed champion in expressing his reluctance was undoubtedly Chief Justice Albert H. Ellett of the Utah Supreme Court. Two examples:

Dyett v. Turner (1968):

We feel like galley slaves chained to our oars by a power from which we cannot free ourselves, but like the slaves of old we think we must cry out when we see the boat heading for the maelstrom directly ahead of us. . . . When we bare our legal backs to receive the verbal lashes, we will try to be brave.

Salt Lake City v. Piepenburg (1977):

It would appear that such an argument ought only to be advanced by depraved, mentally deficient, mind-warped queers. Judges who seek to find technical excuses to permit such pictures to be shown under the pretense of finding some intrinsic value to it are reminiscent of a dog that returns to his vomit in search of some morsel in that filth which may have some redeeming value to his own taste.

. . . .

The opinions of appellate courts are summarized by the publishers in brief "headnotes." Headnotes are assigned a "key number" by the leading law publisher, so that rulings on similar issues can be easily located. Law librarian Tom Woxland estimates there are twelve and a half million headnotes in various legal digests so far. While even the most voracious reader would not seek out headnotes as a source of entertainment, there are some gems to be found:

Courts 106: Preparation and filing of opinions.

An opinion in prose
The law does not demand,
For judicial pronouncement may in poetry be
If that suits the judge's hand;
Metrical line is not perverse
and rhyme will do just fine.
Brown v. State

Animals 44: Civil liability for killing or injuring animals.

If one person's ox kills another person's ox the live ox is to be sold and the proceeds thereof, as well as the dead ox, are to be divided equally between them.
Carriers Ins. Co. v. American Policyholders Ins. Co., citing Exodus 21:35

Constitutional Law 76: Executive powers and functions; nature and scope in general.

Federal bureaucracy is legally permitted to execute congressional mandate with high degree of befuddlement as long as it acts no more befuddled than Congress must reasonably have anticipated.
American Petroleum Institute v. Knecht

. . . .

Some courts have dealt deftly with the problem of their own inconsistency. In *Knuth v. Murphy,* Justice Matson of the Minnesota Supreme Court declared:

Upon [this] issue, this court has displayed extraordinary impartiality by aligning itself on both sides of the question.

And in *People v. Webb,* Justice Richard H. Sims III of the California Court of Appeal confessed:

The good coming of all this is the knowledge that, having taken all conceivable sides on the issue, I must certainly at some point have been right. Unfortunately, it too obviously follows that at some point I must also have been wrong.

. . . .

While Justice Oliver Wendell Holmes of the U.S. Supreme Court was known as the "great dissenter," Justice Michael Musmanno of the Pennsylvania Supreme Court deserves recognition as the "persistent" dissenter. In *Bosley v. Andrews,* the court addressed a dispute between neighboring farmers:

. . . the cows of the Dale Andrews farm in West Salem, Mercer County, were not satisfied to browse and chew their cuds in their own pasture. They were certain that in the fields across the highway, which bordered their owner's domain, the grass was greener, the earth fresher, the trees shadier, and the skies above bluer. Thus from time to time they would leave their own preserves and invade the Bosley farm on the other side of the road where, with spirit of bovine buccaneers, they devoured their neighbor's corn and wheat, destroyed his vegetable gardens, knocked over young peach trees, damaged the apple orchard, mangled berry bushes, and eventually departed, leaving behind them a wide swath of ruin and destruction.

On the morning of April 10, 1950, the cows struck again, were rebuffed, and when they returned for noon lunch, they brought protector, the 1500-pound Hereford white-faced bull.

Mr. Hereford and Mrs. Bosley came face to face. The Hereford charged, Mrs. Bosley screamed, turned to run, stumbled and fell, then fainted. The family collie ran off the bull, and Mrs. Bosley was rescued. A doctor said she suffered an attack of coronary insufficiency and some heart failure.

While upholding a claim for damages to her property, the majority rejected any recovery for Mrs. Bosley's injuries. Justice Musmanno protested, "I shall continue to dissent from it until the cows come home."

. . . .

The plaintiff sued a Mexican restaurant, claiming injuries from a one-inch chicken bone negligently left in a chicken enchilada. His chief obstacle, however,

"Very dramatic, counselor, but the decision stands, even if you don't."

was a fifty-year-old precedent of the California Supreme Court, *Mix v. Ingersoll Candy Co.*, which held that a plaintiff injured by a chicken bone in a chicken pot pie could not recover because the bone was "natural to the type of meat served." On appeal from dismissal of his suit, the court of appeal held that *Mix* could not be distinguished. Justice Marc Poche concurred, but urged the California Supreme Court to reconsider its *Mix* decision:

I concur fully but I write separately to stress my concern with the present state of the chicken bone law. In the recently decided case of *Evart v. Suli,* which our Supreme Court has declined to hear or alternatively to depublish, my colleagues in the second district have valiantly preserved a cause of action for a consumer injured by a piece of beef bone inside a hamburger patty. They have done so by reading *Mix v. Ingersoll Candy Co.* to impose a two-prong test for liability. As the *Evart* court reads *Mix* the injured consumer who bites into prepared food and encounters a substance natural to that food can state a cause of action only if he can also show that it was not common knowledge that such prepared food might contain such an item and that it was an injury which he could not have reasonably guarded against.

We might have attempted to follow the lead of the *Evart* decision and inquire here whether it is a matter of common knowledge that chicken enchiladas might contain bones. Apart from the intellectual thrill of chasing an analysis over such legal fences to achieve the laudable goal of capturing a cause of action for the injured eater, such analysis is silly. There is no sensible distinction to be drawn between chicken bones in chicken enchiladas and chicken bones in chicken pies, unless we begin speculating on whether the reasonable man expects chicken in one to be shredded and chicken in the other to be cut. The problem here is not a lack of distinguishing facts. The problem is that *Mix* is wrongly decided in light of the modern law of products liability. That case is ripe for reconsideration by our Supreme Court. Until and unless that occurs I will explain to my luncheon companions why for sound legal reasons they should order a hamburger and pass up the chicken enchiladas.

. . . .

Consider the dilemma faced by Judge H. Sol Clark of the Georgia Court of Appeals. Called upon to decide an appeal by a man convicted of breaking into the sheriff's office in the county courthouse and stealing eight pistols and five shotguns, Judge Clark could not find a plain English word to appropriately describe the brazen gall such a crime requires. But he found the word he needed in the classic Yiddish expression "chutzpah." He cited the definition offered by Leo Rosten in *The Joys of Yiddish:*

The classic definition of "chutzpah" is that quality enshrined in a man who, having killed his mother and father, throws himself upon the mercy of the court because he is an orphan.

Judge Clark's precedential use of this Yiddish phrase in *Williams v. State* has since been followed, and one can now collect a string of cases competing for the most monumental display of audacity by simply running "chutzpah" through LEXIS or WESTLAW computer programs for legal research. (The word has not yet been assigned a key number.) Our nomination for the winner of this competition is *State v. Strickland,* by Chief Judge Gilbert of the Maryland Court of Special Appeals. Confronted with a defendant who, having been convicted of paying a $2,500 bribe to a judge, sought to have his $2,500 refunded to him, Chief Judge Gilbert concluded that "for whatever else he may lack, [the defendant] suffers not for lack of *chutzpah.*"

. . . .

Judges have been known to apply Yiddish labels to each other, on occasion. The most famous example is Justice Robert Thompson's classic footnote 2 in *People v. Arno.* Presented with a kvetching dissent, Justice Thompson spelled out his response in unusual form. The first letter of each sentence forms the word "schmuck":

We feel compelled by the nature of the attack in the dissenting opinion to spell out a response:
1. Some answer is required to dissent's charge.
2. Certainly we do not endorse "victimless crime."
3. How that question is involved escapes us.
4. Moreover, the constitutional issue is significant.
5. Ultimately it must be addressed in light of precedent.
6. Certainly the course of precedent is clear.
7. Knowing that our result is compelled.

The German definition of "schmuck" is "jewel." The Yiddish definition is somewhat less flattering although equally treasured by some, referring to the male reproductive organ.

. . . .

Two accused robbers in Scotland urged the court to let their guilt or innocence be decided according to a 900-year-old law providing for trial by combat. The brothers asked to take on a "royal champion" and were dismayed to learn that this method of settling disputes had been abolished in 1819.

. . . .

8

POETIC JUSTICE

"In law, what plea so tainted and corrupt
But, being seasoned with a gracious voice,
Obscures the show of evil?"
  WILLIAM SHAKESPEARE, MERCHANT OF VENICE
                                    (III, ii, 74)

Poetic justice: a lawyer with his tongue cut out.
                                    ANONYMOUS

Judge Thomas MacBride was presented with an appeal by a defendant who was fined $150 for nudity in a public park. The defendant objected that he simply removed his wet clothes in an "almost deserted" parking lot. Unfortunately, the defendant neglected to present a proper record of the trial proceedings. Judge MacBride responded with a limerick:

> *There was a defendant named Irving*
> *Who found his conviction unnerving*
> *But with a record that's bare*
> *It's impossible to declare*
> *Whether Irving's appeal is deserving.*

. . . .

Michigan Appellate Court Judge John H. Gillis combined reason and rhyme to uphold the dismissal of a lawsuit about a "beautiful oak" defaced by defendant's automobile. The driver had paid the medical claim ($550 to the tree surgeon for a bark uplift and reconstruction) but plaintiff wanted another $15,000 for pain and suffering.

The court rendered its decision in *Fisher v. Lowe:*

> *We thought that we would never see*
> *A suit to compensate a tree.*
> *A suit whose claim in tort is prest*
> *Upon a mangled tree's behest;*
> *A tree whose battered trunk was prest*
> *Against a Chevy's crumpled crest;*
> *A tree that faces each new day*

With bark and limb in disarray;
A tree that may forever bear
A lasting need for loving care.
Flora lovers though we three,
We must uphold the court's decree.
Affirmed.

. . . .

Judge H. Sol Clark of the Georgia Court of Appeals rendering judgment in *Banks v. State:*

Literary license allows an avid alliterationist authority to postulate parenthetically that the predominating principles presented here may be summarized thusly: Preventing public pollution permits promiscuous perusal of personality but persistent perspicacious patron persuasively provided pertinent perdurable preponderating presumption precedent preventing prison.

And Justice Griffin for the California Court of Appeal in the 1959 lawsuit of *Barendregt v. Downing:*

The peregrinations of the participants in the catawamptious procedure here presented convince this court that the cognomen "mistrial" is an applicable verity.

. . . .

In *Jenkins v. Commissioner,* one Harold Jenkins (better known as Conway Twitty) struggled with the I.R.S. about a certain disallowed business deduction.

The Honorable Leo H. Irwin of the U.S. Tax Court
rescued Twitty in an opinion that concluded with an
"Ode to Conway Twitty":

Twitty Burger went belly up
But Conway remained true,
He repaid his investors, one and all,
It was the moral thing to do.
His fans would not have liked it,
It could have hurt his fame
Had any investors sued him
Like Merle Haggard or Sonny James.
When it was time to file taxes
Conway thought what he would do
Was deduct those payments as a
* business expense*
Under section one-sixty-two.
In order to allow these deductions,
Goes the argument of the Commissioner,
The payments must be ordinary and necessary
To a business of the petitioner.
Had Conway not repaid the investors
His career would have been under cloud,
Under the unique facts of this case
Held: The deductions are allowed.

Refusing to be upstaged, of course, the I.R.S. bowed
to the judicial ruling but with its own response in verse:

Business, the court held,
It's deductible they feel;
We disagree with the answer
But let us not appeal.

. . . .

Some of our robed brethren seem unable to resist penning puns in the body of their opinion. Chief Judge John R. Brown of the U.S. Circuit Court had before him a case challenging certain environmental regulations of the detergent industry. In *Chemical Specialties Mfr. Assoc. v. Clark,* he was decidedly discursive:

As soap, now displaced by latter day detergents, is the grist of Madison Avenue, I add these few comments in the style of that street to indicate my full agreement with the opinion of the court and to keep the legal waters clear and phosphate-free. . . .

Clearly, the decision represents a **Gamble** since we risk a **Cascade** of criticism from an increasing **Tide** of ecology-minded citizens . . . Inspired by the legendary valor of **Ajax,** who withstood Hector's lance, we have **Boldly** chosen the course of uniformity in reversing the lower court's decision upholding Dade County's local labeling laws. . . .

Congress, of course, has the **Cold Power** to preempt . . . Indeed Congress intended to wield its **Arm and Hammer** to **Wisk** away such local regulations and, further, to preclude the growing trend toward this proliferation of individual community supervision . . .

In making this determination, the court is furnished with a **Lever** by our **Brothers** of the Second Circuit. *Chemical Specialties Manufacturer Association v. Lowery, supra.* And so we hold. This is all that need be said. It is as plain as **Mr. Clean** the proper **Action** is that the Dade County Ordinance must be superseded, as **All** comes out in the wash.

. . . .

The federal district court in Pennsylvania holds its own record for writing an entire three-page opinion *(Mackensworth v. American Trading)*, plus footnotes, in verse. Excerpts follow:

A seaman, with help of legal sages,
Sued a shipowner for his wages.
The defendant, in New York City
  (Where served was process without pity)
Thought the suit should fade away,
Since it was started in Pa.
We do not yet rest our inquiry,
  for as is a judge's bent,
We must look to see if there is precedent.
And we found one written in '68 by three big
  wheels
On the Third Circuit Court of Appeals.
In Kane, a ship came but once to
  pick up stores
And hired as agents to do its chores
  a firm of local stevedores.
Since the court upheld service on
  the agents,
  the case is nearly on all fours,
And to defendant's statutory argument
  Kane closes the doors.
So, while trial counsel are doubtless
  in fine fettle,
With many fine fish in their trial kettle,
We urge them not to test their mettle,
Because, for the small sum involved,
  it makes more sense to settle.
In view of the foregoing Opinion,
  at this time

"All rise and welcome ol' Judge Chace./Jurisprudence with a human face."

We enter the following Order,
also in rhyme.

Order

Finding that service of process is bona fide,
The motion to dismiss is hereby denied.
So that this case can now get about its ways,
Defendant shall file an answer within 21 days.

. . . .

Justice Arthur Gilbert of the California Court of Appeal suggests that motions would make much more interesting reading if lawyers adopted the literary style of his favorite novelists. Some examples of how a motion for a continuance might be phrased:

ERNEST HEMINGWAY

It was busy and there was commotion. I looked out the window where the wind touched the top of the trees and far below, the street, white from the sunlight, and the cars inching forward, but I could feel up here that it would not be good, but there was nothing one could do. Pilar, my secretary, looked at me and her eyes told me that this was as bad as when the bulls are running toward you and there is nowhere to climb and you know you will be trampled, but you know that until they do you can live a good life, a short, happy life. And when I asked her for the file and she said, "What file, Ingles?" I knew that the bulls were loose and there was nowhere to go; there was no yesterday, no tomorrow, but that was then and now is here, Your Honor. There was a time when it was good, but now it is a time when it is bad and you can make it good again, and if you can't, it's a rotten shame.

T.S. ELIOT

Thirty days to answer.
It's the cruelest month.
Dead, dying decay, an apt description
For my brain, withered, not resplendent now,
A supplicant, having been etherized upon a table
During the time to answer.
I ask for relief,
Not with a bang, but a whimper.

JAMES JOYCE

HelpmeohGod Time is creptupandI saidyesohheyesyes-
yesyesI need relief nowfromignominious default default
fault-d de fault is mine ohhelptheteatiscaughtinthe-
proceduralwringer. Relief.

WILLIAM FAULKNER

Benji had taken the file and went along the fence with
it and lost it through the spaces in the fence where the
flowers were curling. That's what they said. I started to
cry. Caddy, who smelled like trees, and Quentin, who
just smelled, came to find the file, but I didn't holler
'til mother shouted at Dilsey for bringing me cheap store
cake. Dilsey took me up to bed. Quentin told Caddy he
had to answer. He had to find the file. Caddy did not
know that Benji had taken the file, and Benji could not
know that he had taken the file, because this motion is
written from Benji's point of view, and his IQ is 17.

．．．．．．．．．．．．．．．．

Judges don't hold the corner on poetic incantations.
Inspired by a client he represented on a criminal

charge, lawyer-poet Robert J. Lifton of Chicago
penned:

My Client

Who came to me with tearful eyes,
  with wringing hands and piteous sighs
  and swore the charges were all lies?
  My Client.

Who promised me while still in jail,
  that if I got him out on bail
  my fee he'd pay and would not fail?
  My Client.

Who caused me endless pain and grief,
  and gave me almost no relief
  from statements far beyond belief?
  My Client.

But when at last we'd won the game
  (the jury absolved him from all blame),
  who shook my hand and praised my name?
  My Client.

Then who, despite my earnest plea,
  laughed at me and sneered with glee,
  declined to pay my modest fee?
  My Client.

Who, when I get into the mood,
  will be repaid for acts so rude,
  and get his ass . . . soundly sued?
  My Client.

. . . .

Bankruptcy Judge A. Jay Cristol of Florida, in deny-
ing his own "sua sponte" motion to dismiss the case of
In Re Love, was inspired by Edgar Allan Poe's "The
Raven":

Once upon a midnight dreary, while I pondered weak
  and weary
Over many quaint and curious files of chapter seven
  lore,
While I nodded nearly napping, suddenly there came a
  tapping
As of someone gently rapping, rapping at my chamber
  door.
"Tis some debtor," I muttered, "tapping at my chamber
  door—
Only this and nothing more."
Ah distinctly I recall, it was in the early fall
And the file still was small.
The Code provided I could use it
If someone tried to substantially abuse it.
No party asked that it be heard.
"Sua sponte" whispered a small black bird.
The bird himself, my only maven, strongly looked to be
  a raven.
Upon the words the bird had uttered
I gazed at all the files cluttered.
"Sua sponte," I recall, had no meaning, none at all.
And the cluttered files' sprawl, drove a thought into my
  brain.
Eagerly I wished the morrow—vainly I had sought to
  borrow

From BAFJA, surcease of sorrow—and an order quick
and plain
That this case would not remain as a source of further
pain.
The procedure, it seemed plain.
As the case grew older, I perceived I must be bolder.
And must sua sponte act, to determine every fact,
If primarily consumer debts, are faced,
Perhaps this case is wrongly placed.
This is a thought that I must face: Perhaps I should
dismiss this case.
I moved sua sponte to dismiss it for I knew I would
not miss it.
The Code said I could, I knew it.
But not exactly how to do it, or perhaps someday I'd
rue it.
I leaped up and struck my gavel
For the mystery to unravel.
Could I? Should I? Sua sponte, grant my motion to
dismiss?
While it seemed the thing to do, suddenly I thought of
this:
Looking, looking towards the future and to what there
was to see,
If my motion, it was granted and an appeal came to be,
Who would be the appellee?
Surely, it would not be me.
Who would file, but pray tell me, a learned brief for
the appellee?
The District Judge would not do so,
At least this much I do know.
Tell me raven, how to go.
As I with the ruling wrestled
In the statute I saw nestled

A presumption with a flavor clearly in the debtor's
favor.
No evidence had I taken,
Sua sponte appeared foresaken.
Now my motions caused me terror,
A dismissal would be error.
Upon consideration of §707(b), in anguish, loud I cried
"The court's sua sponte motion to dismiss under
§707(b) is denied."

. . . .

In the state of Washington, there was a dispute about a statute literally requiring judges to wear silk robes. Several Seattle lawyers filed a class action—on April 1—against all state judges, alleging a violation of the "fabric of the law." Their pleadings came in verse:

Come now two members of the Bar
with proper indignation
to make what each is certain are
material allegations.

Each judge and justice of the court,
Supreme, Superior, or Appeal,
is legally required to sport
a gown of silk that's real.

No judge in Rayon merits awe,
it goes beyond aesthetics;
the very fabric of the law
is slandered by synthetics.

And, wherefore, having made their case,
relators now petition
the court to end this dark disgrace
by Writ of Prohibition.

The justices did their homework and studied code section 2.04.110. They ruled against the plaintiffs:

Here's the rule
for the gowns we wear
as cases we decide.
Silk and synthetics?
The same, we declare.
Petition is denied.

· · · · · · · · · · · · · · ·

A poetically inspired plaintiff's counsel in Texas filed his lawsuit "ad-verse" to the defendant:

Defendant proximately caused
said wreck,
Through negligence
in this respect:
Her lookout was bad;
Her right-of-way sad;
Her speed was great;
Her brakes were late.

· · · · · · · · · · · · · · ·

Clever counsel from Riverside, California, Joseph Peter Myers, found himself representing a client in a

"Roses are red,
Your hands as well.
the jury finds you
Guilty as hell."

"bad burger" case involving one of our more famous fast-food eating establishments. His pleadings read in part:

> In need of starch, it was in March, upon the twenty-
>   eighth day,
> Plaintiff herein directed his feet to defendants'
>   burger play.
> The year of 1983 is surely not antique,
> Yet on that day and in that year an "old fashioned"
>   burger did he seek.
> He purchased a doubleburger and a drink,
>   he thought about some fries.
> (It seems that the transaction was really most unwise.)
> Then plaintiff (trusting soul is he)
>   commenced the stuff to eat,
> And found that his new hamburger
>   was really not too sweet.
> In odor it was somewhat odd,
>   in flavor somewhat worse;
> And plaintiff soon suspected that
>   his burger had been cursed.
> (This scene was not from Hamlet,
>   where royal persons plot in;
> But thoughts of Danish intrigue came,
>   for something sure seemed rotten.)
> This magic stuff, which formed a breach
>   of warranty and promise,
> Is something all agree, in food,
>   should be kept farthest from us.
> Some like pickles, some like relish,
>   some say, "Hold 'em, please."
> But plaintiff never, ever said,
>   "I'd like some mousie and some cheese."

Yes, it was mousemeat,
  broiled and ground,
Which plaintiff's tummy
  did surround.
And whose taste he could not manage,
Which caused the soon-to-be-shown damage.
And, of course, defendants failed,
  most carelessly (it seems to me),
To keep meat free of hairy guest
  which then was pressed
Upon the plaintiff, unsuspecting,
Causing trauma, still affecting.
WHEREFORE, plaintiff seeks judgment against
  defendants
Of whose products he took swallows,
  as follows:
1. For general damages, forsooth, and
2. For special damages, in accord with proof,
3. For costs of suit and, we trust,
4. Such further relief as the court deems just.

. . . .

When Judge Jerry Buchmeyer delayed releasing his
ruling in *Shafer v. A.A.F.E.S.*, impatient counsel hired
a messenger to deliver a singing telegram, sung to the
tune of "Let It Snow, Let It Snow, Let It Snow":

> *Oh the case is Shafer v. AAFES,*
> *We recall the trial you gave us,*
> *Do you remember, yes or no?*
>   *Let us know*
>   *Let us know*
>   *Let us know.*

Oh the age of this case is gallful,
Your procastination awful,
Our impatience we must show:
   Let us know
   Let us know
   Let us know.
Would you finally give the word
Now we're down on our knees, pretty please?
And we heard from a little bird
You'll even add an attorney's fees.
Oh we've spoken as long as we dare to,
One final question have we for you,
Are we shafted, yes or no?
   Let us know
   Let us know
   Let us know.

· · · · · · · · · · · · · ·

Some defendants wax eloquent; some do not. A bank robber in Tennessee handed a teller the following note:

Watch out. This a rubbery. I have an oozy traned on your but. Dump the in a sack, this one. No die pakkets or other triks or I will tare you a new naval. No kwarter with red stuff on them too.

· · · · · · · · · · · · · ·

9

SUPREME FOLLY

"We are not final because we are infallible; but we are infallible only because we are final."
JUSTICE ROBERT H. JACKSON, BROWN V. ALLEN.

"Some men achieve insignificance; others have insignificance thrust upon them."
PROFESSOR FRANK H. EASTERBROOK

Chief Justice John Marshall, who presided over the U.S. Supreme Court from 1801 until 1835, established a tradition of serving wine during conferences of the justices, but only if it was a rainy day. On one occasion, Marshall asked Justice Joseph Story to "step to the window and see if it doesn't look like rain." When Justice Story reported the sun was shining brightly, Chief Justice Marshall noted, "Our jurisdiction is so vast that it must be raining somewhere," and ordered the wine brought out.

. . . .

Justice Thomas Johnson of Maryland sat on the U.S. Supreme Court for two years, from 1791 to 1793. During this period, the court had no cases to decide. Justice Johnson did write a letter of resignation, however, citing his disinclination to "undertake the labor."

. . . .

Chief Justice Charles Evans Hughes was ready to convene the Court when he realized that Justice James C. McReynolds was missing. He sent a messenger to locate McReynolds and tell him to hurry. McReynolds, noted for his independence, sent the messenger back with his own message: "Justice McReynolds says to tell you that he doesn't work for you."

. . . .

Over the course of two centuries, the style and tone of dissenting opinions has been transformed from apologetic to apoplectic. Consider two examples:

Justice W. Johnson, dissenting in 1807 in *Ex Parte Bollman:*

In this case I have the misfortune to dissent from the majority of my brethren. . . . I feel myself much relieved from the painful sensation resulting from the necessity of dissenting . . . , in being supported by the opinion of one of my brethren.

Justice John Paul Stevens, dissenting in 1977 in *Dobbert v. Florida:*

I assume that [the majority opinion] will ultimately be regarded as nothing more than an archaic gargoyle. It is nonetheless distressing to witness such a demeaning construction of a majestic bulwark in the framework of our Constitution.

. . . .

The nine justices of the Supreme Court seldom agree on a single opinion. Occasionally, so many separate dissenting and concurring opinions are produced that it becomes difficult to sort out the positions being taken. Justice Henry Baldwin, on one occasion in 1838, joined both a majority opinion affirming a judgment, and a dissenting opinion declaring the Court lacked jurisdiction to decide the case.
Beaston v. Farmer's Bank

On a more recent occasion, with apologies to Finley Peter Dunne, James M. Marsh of the Philadelphia bar discovered a unanimous dissent:*

*Reprinted by permission of James M. Marsh and "The Shingle" of the Philadelphia Bar Association. Finley Peter Dunne was a Chicago journalist whose nationally syndicated sketches used the fictional Mr. Dooley to comment in Irish dialect on a broad sweep of national events from 1892 until 1920.

"Everyone of them dissented," said Mr. Dooley. "It was unanimous. They's nine jedges on that coort, and everyone of them dissented—includin' me brother Brennan, who wrote the opinion they're all dissentin' from."

"That don't make sinse," said Mr. Hennessy. "You can't have all the jedges dissentin'—it's impossible."

"Well, it may be impossible, but it happened anyhow," said Mr. Dooley, "and it's printed right here in the Coort's own Joornal of its Proceedings for February 25th.

"Read it for yourself:

"No. 28 James C. Rogers, petitioner v. Missouri Pacific Railroad Company, a Corporation. On writ of certiorari to the Supreme Court of Missouri.

"Judgment reversed with costs and case remanded to the Supreme Court of Missouri for proceedings not inconsistent with the opinion of this Court.

"Opinion by Mr. Justice Brennan.

"Mr. Justice Burton concurs in the result.

"Mr. Justice Reed would affirm the judgment of the Supreme Court of Missouri.

"Mr. Justice Harlan, dissenting in Nos. 28, 42, 59 and concurring in No. 46, filed a separate opinion.

"Mr. Justice Burton concurred in Part I of Mr. Justice Harlan's opinion.

"Mr. Chief Justice Warren, Mr. Justice Black, Mr. Justice Douglas, Mr. Justice Clark, and Mr. Justice Brennan concurred in Part I of Mr. Justice Harlan's opinion except insofar as it disapproves the grant of the writ of certiorari.

"Mr. Justice Frankfurter filed a separate dissenting opinion for Nos. 28, 42, 46, and 50."

"See what I mean," said Mr. Dooley. "Each and ivery one of them dissented in this No. 28, called Rogers varsus the Missouri Pacific. Even Brennan, J., who wrote the opinion for the Court. He signed Harlan's dissent. Me old friend Holmes would've sooner been caught with a split writ than to show up on both sides of a case like that . . .

"I tell ye, Hennessy, it's a demoralizin' situation. Here's the highest coort in the land, and they're all half right but none of them are all right and they're tellin' on each other at that."

"But what about me friend Stanley Reed?" asked Mr. Hennessy. "He didn't sign anybody else's opinion, did he?"

"No, he was the smart wan," said Mr. Dooley. "He quit."

"He *quit?*" said Mr. Hennessy. "Just like *that?*"

"Just like that," said Mr. Dooley. "He voted loud and clear to back up the Supreme Court of Missouri—and then he quit."

"On February 25th he did it, right after they handed down this Rogers case. He walked out of that court that same day and he hasn't been back since."

"Well," said Mr. Hennessy, "I don't blame him, I'd quit too."

"That's the trouble with thim jedges, though," said Mr. Dooley.

"What's that?" asked Mr. Hennessey.

"They don't quit often enough," said Mr. Dooley.

. . . .

Justices are occasionally put in the awkward position of "eating their words," having to explain why a prior position they themselves espoused must now be rejected. A classic example of accomplishing this with grace and humor is the opinion of Justice Robert H. Jackson in *McGrath v. Kristensen:*

I concur in the judgment and opinion of the court. But since it is contrary to an opinion which, as Attorney General, I rendered in 1940, I owe some word of explanation. I am entitled to say of that opinion what any discriminating reader must think of it—that it was as foggy as the statute the Attorney General was asked to interpret. . . .

Precedent, however, is not lacking for ways by which a judge may recede from a prior opinion that has proven untenable and perhaps misled others. . . . Baron Bramwell extricated himself from a somewhat similar embarrassment by saying, "The matter does not appear to me now as it appears to have appeared to me then." And Mr. Justice Story, accounting for his contradiction of his own former opinion, quite properly put the matter: "My own error, however, can furnish no ground for its being adopted by this court. . . ." Perhaps Dr. Johnson really went to the heart of the matter when he explained a blunder in his dictionary—"Ignorance, sir, ignorance." But an escape less self-deprecating was taken by Lord Westbury, who, it is said, rebuffed a barrister's reliance upon an earlier opinion of his Lordship: "I can only say that I am amazed that a man of my intelligence should have been guilty of giving such an opinion." If there are other ways of gracefully and good-naturedly surrendering former views to a better considered position, I invoke them all.

· · · · · · · · · · · · · · ·

In offering advice for lawyers preparing to present arguments to the Supreme Court, Justice Robert H. Jackson cautioned them against flattering the justices. "We think well enough of ourselves already," he explained.

· · · · · · · · · · · · · · ·

At the turn of the century, a young lawyer from Kansas appeared before the court to argue an important case on the land rights of Indian tribes. Mr. Justice Brewer, the recognized authority on Indian law, interrupted his argument to ask, "Counsellor, what do *you* think the status of an allottee is?" The lawyer threw both hands in the air and exclaimed in frustration, "If you fellows up there don't know, how do you think us fellows down here should know?"

. . . .

Justice Holmes regularly began an oral argument in the Supreme Court by inquiring what jurisdiction the Court had over the case. Rather than ask about each of the statutory alternatives available to bring a case before the Court, he simply asked, "How did you get here?" On one occasion, a young lawyer from Ohio responded, "By the B. & O. Railroad, Your Honor."

. . . .

Before his appointment to the U.S. Supreme Court, Justice Holmes presided over the Supreme Court of Massachusetts. On one occasion, an attorney named Swasey appeared to seek a continuance of a murder case. Justice Holmes responded,

Mr. Swasey, the record shows that the trial of this case has at your request been continued once. Last summer, when I was in England visiting the law courts, Mr. Justice Stephen commented to me on the importance of speedy trials in the administration of justice, particularly in capital cases while witnesses were available, evidence fresh in the mind, and before suggestions could create false psychological memories.

As Holmes paused before ruling, Swasey inquired, "Has Your Honor read the morning papers?" Holmes inquired what bearing the morning papers would have on his motion. "None," replied Swasey, "but they do report that yesterday Mr. Justice Stephen was judicially committed to an institution for the feeble-minded." The continuance was granted.

· · · · · · · · · · · · · · ·

Justice William O. Douglas frequently brought a stack of books and papers with him to oral arguments. On one occasion, Justice Harry Blackmun watched Douglas writing furiously behind a mound of books while oral arguments were being presented in a different case. He passed Justice Douglas a note, saying, "Bill, what are you doing, writing another opinion during the middle of oral arguments?" Douglas wrote a note in return, saying, "Yes, this lawyer was done 20 minutes ago, but he didn't know it."

· · · · · · · · · · · · · · ·

Justice Douglas was well known for his love of western country music. He delighted in recounting the titles of his favorite songs. Among them were, "When the Phone Don't Ring, You'll Know It's Me," "Walk

"The Honorable Justice Feltcher will now deliver a dissent."

Out Backwards, So I'll Think You're Coming In," and "My Wife Ran Off with My Best Friend, and I Sure Do Miss Him." These gems were found in an album entitled "Songs I Learned at My Mother's Knee, and at Other Joints."

. . . .

The late Edward Bennett Williams once recounted a lesson learned from Justice William O. Douglas:

Mr. Justice Douglas publicly observed on one occasion that the most important distinction impressed upon him in his days as a Columbia law student was the difference between a schnook and schlemiel. He said a schnook is a fellow who gets dressed up in his dinner jacket and goes to a very elegant dinner party and and proceeds to spill the soup, and spill the gravy from the entree, and then slobber the chocolate sauce when the dessert is served. The schlemiel is the fellow he spills it on. It has been my experience that in every case involving twenty or more defense lawyers on the criminal side of the court we are apt to draw one or more schnooks, and it makes all the rest of us into schlemiels.

Actually, Justice Douglas may have confused the schnook with the schlimazel. The difference between a schlemiel and the schlimazel was summed up in *Dictionary Schmictionary!* (by Paul Hoffman and Matt Freedman) as follows:

The *schlemiel* brings on his own misfortune, unlike the *schlimazel* who gets it handed to him. For example, when a *schlimazel* drops a piece of buttered toast, it always lands buttered side down. But when a *schlemiel* drops a piece of toast, he has buttered both sides.

The *schnook* is probably more closely related to the *schlimazel* than the *schlemiel*. It's easy to get them confused, as they frequently travel in pairs.

. . . .

In presenting oral argument against the admission of hypnotically refreshed testimony, the Arkansas attorney general repeatedly referred to the testimony of a neuropsychologist as a "psycho-psychologist." Finally, Justice Antonin Scalia interrupted his argument to inquire, "What is a psycho-psychologist? A psychologist with a stutter?"

. . . .

While serving on the court of appeals, Justice Scalia was called upon to decide whether regulations promulgated by the secretary of agriculture for changing labeling requirements for meat products were properly adopted. He began his scholarly opinion with tongue firmly in cheek:

This case, involving legal requirements for the content and labeling of meat products such as frankfurters, affords a rare opportunity to explore simultaneously both parts of Bismarck's aphorism that "No man should see how laws or sausages are made."

Community Nutrition Institute v. Block

. . . .

Chief Justice William Rehnquist is known to be very strict in enforcing time limits at oral argument, stopping lawyers in the middle of a one-syllable word when the red signal light appears on the podium. On one occasion, the lawyer saw the red light come on and stopped voluntarily. Justice Antonin Scalia observed, "He wasn't watching. I think you could have gotten away with the end of that sentence." Chief Justice Rehnquist responded, "Even Homer nodded."

. . . .

Among the names of the famous and infamous enshrined in U.S. Supreme Court opinions are the names of 89 baseball players put there by Justice Harry Blackmun. In deciding the case of *Flood v. Kuhn,* which challenged the "reserve clause" in baseball players' contracts, Justice Blackmun also felt inclined to decide which of the thousands of early ballplayers deserved immortality:

Then there are the many names, celebrated for one reason or another, that have sparked the diamond and its environs and that have provided tinder for recaptured thrills, for reminiscence and comparisons, and for conversation and anticipation in-season and off-season: Ty Cobb, Babe Ruth, Tris Speaker, Walter Johnson, Henry Chadwick, Eddie Collins, Lou Gehrig, Grover Cleveland Alexander, Rogers Hornsby, Harry Hooper, Goose Goslin, Jackie Robinson, Honus Wagner, Joe McCarthy, John McGraw, Deacon Phillippe, Rube Marquard, Christy Mathewson, Tommy Leach, Big Ed Delahanty, Davy Jones, Germany Schaefer, King Kelly, Big Dan Brouthers, Wahoo Sam Crawford, Wee Willie Keeler, Big Ed Walsh, Jimmy Austin, Fred Snodgrass, Satchel Paige, Hugh Jennings, Fred Merkle, Iron Man McGinnity, Three-Finger Brown, Harry and Stan Coveleski, Connie Mack, Al Bridwell, Red Ruffing Amos Rusie, Cy Young, Smoky Joe Wood, Chief Meyers, Chief Bender, Bill Klem, Hans Lobert, Johnny Evers, Joe Tinker, Roy Campanella, Miller Huggins, Rube Bressler, Dazzy Vance, Edd Roush, Bill Wambsganass, Clark Griffith, Branch Rickey, Frank Chance, Cap Anson, Nap Lajoie, Sad Sam Jones, Bob O'-Farrell, Lefty O'Doul, Bobby Veach, Willie Kamm, Heinie Groh, Lloyd and Paul Waner, Stuffy McInnis, Charles Comiskey, Roger Bresnahan, Bill Dickey, Zack Wheat, George Sisler, Charlie Gehringer, Eppa Rixey, Harry Heilmann, Fred Clarke, Dizzy Dean, Hank Greenberg, Pie Traynor, Rube Waddell, Bill Terry, Carl Hubbell, Old Hoss Radbourne, Moe Berg, Rabbit Maranville, Jimmie Foxx, Lefty Grove. The list seems endless.

Not surprisingly, two justices dissented from Justice Blackmun's list! While Chief Justice Burger and Justice White refused to join Justice Blackmun's list, they declined to state whether they found it over-inclusive, under-inclusive, or simply irrelevant.

. . . .

In an interview in the *Ladies' Home Journal,* Justice Sandra Day O'Connor was quoted as saying, "I'm the yenta of Paradise Valley. I have introduced a number of couples, including my own sister and brother-in-law." While Yente was the name of the matchmaker in *Fiddler on the Roof,* the Yiddish term "yenta" refers to a blabbermouth. Justice O'Connor may be a matchmaker, but a yenta she's not.

. . . .

An appearance before the California Supreme Court caused momentary embarrassment for an Orange County prosecutor. Deputy District Attorney Thomas J. Borris, arguing in a drug-related death case, at one point addressed the justices as "you guys."

"When you say 'you guys,' to whom are you referring?" Chief Justice Malcolm M. Lucas asked icily.

Justice Joyce L. Kennard, the lone woman on the court, asked, "Does that include me?"

The prosecutor quickly apologized.

. . . .

The highest court of the State of New York is the court of appeal. And the first recorded precedent of the New York Court of Appeal, found at 1 New York 1, is *Pierce v. Delamiter,* in which the court reviewed a judgment rendered by Judge Greene Bronson. Meanwhile, though, Judge Greene Bronson had been appointed a justice of the court of appeal. Thus, the first issue the high court had to decide was whether a justice could sit in review of his own decision. The court ruled:

There is nothing in the nature of things which makes it improper for a judge to sit in review upon his own judgments. If he is what a judge ought to be: wise enough to know he is fallible and therefore ever ready to learn, great and honest enough to discard all mere prior opinion and follow truth wherever it may, and courageous enough to acknowledge his errors, he is then the very best man to sit upon review of his own opinion. He will have the benefit of a double discussion. If right at first he will be confirmed in his opinion, and if wrong, he will be quite as likely to find it out as anyone else.

The court then affirmed the decision of the trial court. The opinion was signed by Justice Greene Bronson.

· · · · · · · · · · · · · · ·

Upon retiring from the U.S. Court of Appeals to return to the practice of law, Judge Thurman Arnold summed up his experience as an appellate judge:

"I'd rather have to talk to a bunch of damn fools than listen to them."

· · · · · · · · · · · · · · ·

10

JUST DESSERTS

"Let the punishment match the offense."
                    CICERO, DE LEGIBUS

"When every case in law is right;
No squire in debt, nor no poor knight;
When slanders do not live in tongues;
Nor cutpurses come not to throngs."
     WILLIAM SHAKESPEARE, KING LEAR (III, ii, 85)

A Burbank, California, judge who demanded punctuality of those attending his courtroom fined himself $25 when he arrived 15 minutes late after lunch. "I just figured I had to teach myself a lesson," he explained.

. . . .

A Des Moines judge found himself locked outside his chambers, along with a defense lawyer and his client—due to be sentenced for burglary. Maintenance workers tried keys and drills but could not open the door. The lawyer volunteered his client—who had it open in three seconds. After thanking him for his services, the judge sentenced him to the maximum ten years in state prison.

. . . .

Justice Robert Gardner of California describes a case which came before him of a "normal, run-of-the-mill burglar" who was sent to prison. While in prison, he took a course in welding and learned how to handle an acetylene torch. Shortly after his release, he was back in court. The charge: safecracking.

. . . .

Excerpts from English Probation Reports:

In a case of a young man caught robbing the elderly . . .

The reparation element of the programme will be centered on the Beauvale Old People's Home. Simon will interview elderly residents and discover what they most miss about the outside world.

Another young robber recommended for training . . .

The course will develop Kevin's confrontational skills and give him the elements of money management.

A burglar back in court for violating the terms of his probation . . .

Terry, like many of his peer group, has been involved in a number of thefts and burglaries since his last court appearance, but has otherwise responded extremely well to his supervision order. I consider that a custodial disposal in this case would be too disruptive to his currently constructive lifestyle. I shall continue to keep him in my close focus.

. . . .

Transcript of an Actual Sentencing in Arizona:

DEFENDANT   But Judge, I can't do 61,500 years!
   JUDGE   Well, just do as much of it as you can. And have a nice day.

. . . .

Another one, from California:
   JUDGE   You stand convicted of murder. Do you have anything to say before this court pronounces sentence?

DEFENDANT As God is my judge, I didn't do it. I'm
           not guilty.
JUDGE   He isn't, I am. You did. You are.

. . . .

A federal trial judge in the Territory of New Mexico,
presiding at Taos in an adobe stable as a temporary
courtroom, put it eloquently in sentencing a man convicted of murder:

José Manuel Miguel Xavier Gonzales, in a few short weeks
it will be spring. The snows of winter will flee away, the
ice will vanish and the air will become soft and balmy. In
short, José Manuel Miguel Xavier Gonzales, the annual mir-
acle of the year's awakening will come to pass . . . But you
won't be here.

The rivulet will run its purring course to the sea, the timid
desert flowers will put forth their tender shoots, the glorious
valleys of the imperial domain will blossom as the rose . . .
Still, you won't be here to see.

From every treetop some wildwoods songster will carol his
mating song, butterflies will sport in the sunshine, the busy
bee will hum happily as it pursues its accustomed vocation,
the gentle breeze will tease the tassels of the wild grasses,
and all nature, José Manuel Miguel Xavier Gonzales, will be
glad but you. You won't be here to enjoy it because I command the sheriff to lead you out to some remote spot, swing
you by the neck from a nodding bough of some sturdy oak,
and let you hang until you are dead.

And then, José Manuel Miguel Xavier Gonzales, I further
command that such officer retire quickly from your dangling
corpse so that the vultures from the heavens may descend

upon it until nothing shall remain but the bare, bleached bones of a cold-blooded, blood-thirsty, throat-cutting, sheepherding, murdering son-of-a-bitch.

. . . .

An attorney-minister mustered the strength of his second profession to collect his fees. In a series of letters, he stated that he had "revelations" from God that the client would suffer biblical curses if he refused to pay. The client reported the lawyer to the state bar for discipline and reprimand.

. . . .

In a criminal appeal, the sole contention presented to Justice Robert Puglia of Sacramento, California, was a complaint that in sentencing the defendant to six years in prison, the trial judge gave him credit for only 234 days of local custody, instead of the 235 days he had actually served. The court ruled:

The judgment is modified to give defendant one additional day of custody credit and the trial court is ordered to amend the abstract of judgment accordingly and to forward forthwith a certified copy of the amended abstract to the Department of Corrections. As amended, the judgment is affirmed. Have a nice day.

. . . .

You just don't mess with legends. A Texas jury convicted an airline baggage handler of theft in his purloining and hocking the Lone Ranger's pistols while the crime fighter was traveling the Texas plains. The defendant appealed his conviction, complaining that the judge permitted the masked man to wear his sunglasses and white hat while testifying. After losing, he was sentenced to 600 hours of cleaning police stables and shoveling manure.

. . . .

In Seattle, it was forty cents' worth of broccoli that led to three years' worth of litigation. A shopper broke stalks off a bunch, paying only for the florets. An irate manager pressed the case and the local prosecutor argued that this behavior was like trying to buy only the pictures in *Playboy* magazine. A jury acquittal didn't end the matter. The market made a $100 civil penalty demand under state law (plus the forty cents). The shopper sued for defamation and malicious prosecution, but the jury deadlocked. All the publicity didn't help the store. Some new shopper walked in, opened a steak package, ripped off the fat, and demanded that the steak be reweighed.

. . . .

A woman traveling to San Francisco by Greyhound bus was visiting the restroom when the bus swerved and her buttocks became lodged in the emergency window. A jury awarded $4,300 in damages for emotional distress after hearing psychiatric testimony.

. . . .

A St. Louis, Missouri, public defender met a client charged with fraudulent use of a credit card in her office. She interrupted the conference to step out for a soft drink. Afterwards, she discovered her wallet was missing. Police arrested the client at a nearby service station where he was trying to use her credit cards.

. . . .

In Salem, Virginia, the lawyer was busy at his desk, awaiting the arrival of his new client to discuss pending drunk driving charges. Suddenly there was an awful crash, and the lawyer found his client sitting in a car that had been driven through the front doors of the law office. A second DWI charge was filed.

. . . .

During an impassioned argument on behalf of his client, a New Jersey attorney swung his arm wide and struck a water pitcher sitting on nearby plaintiff's table. The plaintiff, who had sued the lawyer's client for back injuries suffered in an auto accident, jumped quickly to avoid the spill—apparently reinjuring herself. The judge awarded her damages, but she's back again— suing the lawyer and his partner.

. . . .

A firebrand defense lawyer from Shreveport was representing some clients charged with recklessness in a boating accident. He was out in a boat during a thunderstorm, and suddenly raised his hands heavenward and proclaimed, "Here I am." Within seconds a lighting bolt struck him dead, leaving untouched the other three people in the boat with him.

. . . .

Then there was the handwritten note sent to court-appointed counsel after he sent a younger lawyer to interview the client in jail:

I appreciated you sending Mr. Asand to see me. But, I been talking to my friend who reads law books and he said I should be able to see you. I like Mr. Asand but your secretary said you are a good lawyer and you are the one the judge gave me. Mr. Asand seemed real nice but I want a lawyer that is been around.

I don't want to be nasty but my friend says you has to come see me or else you can get in trouble. My wife works at Krispy Kreme Donuts and I know I don't have to pay you but if you is good I will give you $50.00 for nothing. Thank You.

Sammy

P.S. If you gets me off, I might find some of that monie they says I took.

. . . .

Former South Dakota Governor William Janklow had a policy of not claiming criminal fugitives who were found in California. He considered living in California to be sufficient punishment and gave accused

"Please, Your Honor, not house arrest!"

criminals the choice of prosecution in South Dakota or remaining in California. He wrote to then-Governor Jerry Brown, thanking him for providing a "haven for our outcasts," and adding, "We kind of feel there is a beacon in California saying: 'Give us your felons, your pickpockets, your crooked masses yearning to be free.' "

. . . .

A Vallejo, California, cemetery was sued for $500,-000 by relatives of the deceased, who alleged that workers improperly approached the problem of an undersized grave. When the employees realized the coffin was larger than the excavation, they first attempted to turn it on its side and lower it. But mourners intervened. Then they allegedly tried to break off the handles. When that too failed, they tried to force it by jumping up and down on the lid, causing the coffin to break and the service to be postponed for several days.

. . . .

Relatives at a Fort Lauderdale funeral weren't happy with services rendered to them either. Mourners tripped on artificial turf en route to the gravesite. Pallbearers hired by the funeral home showed up "slovenly attired and unclean." During the middle of the service, a worker interrupted and asked the rabbi to move his car. It got worse. After the rabbi refused, the worker tried to tow the car with a chain and backhoe. As the casket was being lowered, the lid opened, exposing the deceased's foot with a white tag attached. It also didn't fit the vault and workers resorted to iron pry bars in order to remove the support straps.

. . . .

An Abilene, Texas, funeral home was not too pleased to find its Yellow Pages ad listed under "Frozen Foods—Wholesale." The telephone company was sued for over $300,000, the home claiming that it was held up to public ridicule because the ad was not proofread and placed more appropriately under "Funeral Directors." Also alleged were the receipt of numerous crank calls, including a man who asked "what meat was on special for the day."

. . . .

And a funeral may not be a good choice for a robbery. A Florida man robbed about twenty mourners after springing into the mourning room dressed in shorts and sneakers, shouting obscenities and waving a pistol. The thief threatened to shoot the corpse or make them all strip if his demands were not met. A "not guilty by reason of insanity" plea was entered but the robber was convicted. His sentence: 985 years!

. . . .

A gang of robbers in Ireland spent days tunneling 25 yards underground, crawling through sewers and cutting a basement wall to enter a bank. But they emerged in the women's rest room instead of the vault, triggering an alarm. It was a bold venture—they started their tunneling from a vacant lot next to a police building.

. . . .

Two bank thieves, armed with shotguns, burst into an L.A. bank and ordered everyone to lie down on the floor. All employees and customers complied, leaving no one to fetch the money. The robbers hesitated and then fled penniless.

. . . .

A pair of Michigan robbers entered a record shop brandishing revolvers and ordering, "Nobody move." When his partner moved, the second bandit shot him in the head at point-blank range.

. . . .

Nancy Miller of Oroville, California eagerly accepted the invitation to attend a "Neighborhood Watch" meeting at a neighbor's home. She was the victim of a recent burglary in which her TV set, Christmas stockings and a favorite dress had been stolen from a storage locker. As she sat calmly through the presentation by two police officers, she realized why she felt so much at home. Her television set was in a corner, and her stockings were hung by the fireplace. The clincher was that the hostess was wearing her dress. She caught up with the officers outside, and told them what she had seen. They returned with a search warrant, and arrested the host and hostess after recovering $9,000 worth of stolen property. Score one for "Neighborhood Watch!"

. . . .

A San Jose, California, suspect trying to elude police hoped to melt into a crowd for his escape. Turns out it was a police league baseball game. Most of the spectators were cops.

. . . .

An East L.A. bank robber successfully walked out with $1,700 in unmarked bills only to discover that he had locked the keys of his getaway car inside the vehicle.

. . . .

A St. Louis parking garage was stuck up by a man wearing a T-shirt and packing a pistol. Printed across the back of the shirt was the name "James." He was arrested walking a few blocks away, still wearing the shirt.

. . . .

An angry dentist in Oklahoma, whose patient refused to pay for her $600 dentures because of a small misalignment, decided on some self-help repossession.

Curt Brookover arrived at his patient's home and a yelling match ensued. He reached into her mouth to reclaim his product, at which point, he claims, she "bit as hard as she could." When he extracted his fingers, the teeth fell to the ground. Curt says that they both went for them "but I was faster." Patient Lee Ann Stoval denies biting him and claims he "attacked her viciously, hurling her to the ground, twisting her neck, and pulling out the dentures." A suit claiming $530,-000 in damages was filed.

· · · · · · · · · · · · · · ·

A Raleigh man apparently was trying to bring cocaine into the country in his luggage but hesitated when he went to claim it. Officers observed him watching his luggage going round and round on the carousel. Finally the man retrieved someone else's bag and tried to leave. Questioned, he immediately claimed ownership and consented to a search of the bag. He fell silent when it was opened and contained marijuana. Then his own luggage was seized with 10 ounces of cocaine. The true owner of the marijuana was never found.

· · · · · · · · · · · · · · ·

Two culprits parked their old car across from an auto parts store and went in. As one distracted the clerk, the other grabbed a battery from the display case and ran. When apprehended, the men were still trying to install the battery—a display-only model, filled with cardboard.

. . . .

A young purse snatcher met his match with 73-year-old Louise Burt. The retired saleswoman was headed to a bingo game when the snatch occurred. She chased the man six blocks before police officers joined in the pursuit. The suspect jumped off a roof, fell two stories, and broke both ankles. Louise was heard to comment, "He was a little shrimp and I could have cold-cocked him with my fist to his jaw."

. . . .

While serving as Mendocino County, California, district attorney, Joe Allen tangled with the board of supervisors about his annual budget. The following poster abruptly appeared at choice locations around the county:

NOTICE

To All

THIEVES,
THUGS,
CON-MEN
AND
OTHER
CRIMINALS

NOW PRACTICING IN MENDOCINO COUNTY

PLEASE BE ADVISED:

The District Attorney's Office has run out
of funds to prosecute you for your crimes
until July 1, 1982.

THEREFORE:

Please postpone the commission of all
crimes which are not urgent until after
that date.

THANK YOU.

Your consideration is appreciated.

JOSEPH D. ALLEN

11

A CODICIL OF
SPURIOUS PRECEDENTS

"Parodies and caricatures are the most penetrating of criticisms."
    ALDOUS HUXLEY, POINT COUNTER POINT

"We still have judgment here; that we but teach
Bloody instructions, which, being taught, return
To plague the inventor: this even-handed justice
Commends the ingredients of our poisoned chalice
To our own lips."
    WILLIAM SHAKESPEARE, MACBETH (I, vii, 7)

Perhaps it says something about the sense of humor of lawyers and judges, but parody is unquestionably their favorite form. The stilted formalism of judicial opinions and legal scholarship lends itself easily to parody, and the opinions and articles collected here succeed as humor because they seem so real: so real that some of these examples are discussed in actual opinions, and often cited as though they were actual cases. Because they are all fictional, unlike the gospel truth in the remainder of this book, they are separately compiled in this codicil.

. . . .

When Is a Horse a Small Bird?

One of the classic examples of judicial reasoning is, unfortunately, entirely fictional. It was originally published in the *Criminal Law Quarterly* in Canada in 1966.

Regina v. Ojibway*

This is an appeal by the Crown by way of a stated case from a decision of the magistrate acquitting the accused of a charge under the Small Birds Act, R.S.O., 1960, c.724, s.2. The facts are not in dispute. Fred Ojibway, an Indian, was riding his pony through Queen's Park on January 2, 1965. Being impoverished, and having been forced to pledge his saddle, he substituted a downy pillow in lieu of the said saddle. On this particular day the accused's misfortune was

*Published originally in 8 Crim. Law Q. 137 (1965–66). Reproduced with permission of Mr. Hart Pomerantz and Canada Law Book, Inc., 240 Edward St., Aurora, Ontario, Canada L4G 3S9.

further heightened by the circumstance of his pony breaking its right foreleg. In accord with current Indian custom, the accused then shot the pony to relieve it of its awkwardness.

The accused was then charged with having breached the Small Birds Act, s.2 of which states:

2. Anyone maiming, injuring, or killing small birds is guilty of an offense and subject to a fine not in excess of two hundred dollars.

The learned magistrate acquitted the accused, holding, in fact, that he had killed his horse and not a small bird. With respect, I cannot agree.

In light of the definition section my course is quite clear. Section 1 defines "bird" as "a two-legged animal covered with feathers." There can be no doubt that this case is covered by this section.

Counsel for the accused made several ingenious arguments to which, in fairness, I must address myself. He submitted that the evidence of the expert clearly concluded that the animal in question was a pony and not a bird, but this is not the issue. We are not interested in whether the animal in question is a bird or not in fact, but whether it is one in law. Statutory interpretation has forced many a horse to eat birdseed for the rest of its life.

Counsel also contended that the neighing noise emitted by the animal could not possibly be produced by a bird. With respect the sounds emitted by an animal are irrelevant to its nature, for a bird is no less a bird because it is silent.

Counsel for the accused also argued that since there was evidence to show accused had ridden the animal, this pointed to the fact that it could not be a bird but was actually a pony. Obviously, this avoids the issue. The issue is not whether the animal was ridden or not, but whether it was shot or not, for to ride a pony or a bird is of no offense at all. I believe that counsel now sees his mistake.

Counsel contends that the iron shoes found on the animal decisively disqualify it from being a bird. I must inform counsel, however, that how an animal dresses is of no concern to this court.

Counsel relied on the decision in *Re Chickadee*, where he contends that in similar circumstances the accused was acquitted. However, this is a horse of a different color. A close reading of that case indicates that the animal in question there was not a small bird, but, in fact, a midget of a much larger species. Therefore, that case is inapplicable to our facts.

Counsel finally submits that the word "small" in the title "Small Birds Act" refers not to "Birds" but to "Act," making it "The Small Act Relating to Birds." With respect, counsel did not do his homework very well, for the Large Birds Act, R.S.O., 1960, c.725, is just as small. If pressed, I need only refer to the Small Loans Act, R.S.O., 1960, c.727, which is twice as large as the Large Birds Act.

It remains then to state my reason for judgment, which, simply, is as follows: Different things may take on the same meaning for different purposes. For the purpose of the Small Birds Act, all two-legged, feather-covered animals are birds. This, of course, does not imply that only two-legged animals qualify, for the legislative intent is to make two legs merely the minimum requirement. The statute therefore contemplated multi-legged animals with feathers as well. Counsel submits that having regard to the purpose of the statute only small animals "naturally covered" with feathers could have been contemplated. However, had this been the intention of the legislature, I am certain that the phrase "naturally covered" would have been expressly inserted just as "Long" was inserted in the "Longshoreman's" Act.

Therefore, a horse with feathers on its back must be deemed for the purposes of this Act to be a bird, and, *a fortiori,* a pony with feathers on its back is a small bird.

Counsel posed the following rhetorical question: If the pillow had been removed prior to the shooting, would the animal still be a bird? To this let me answer rhetorically: Is a bird any less of a bird without its feathers?

. . . .

Among the cases which found *Regina v. Ojibway* a useful precedent was the decision of the Court of Appeals of Kentucky in *R. J. Stevens v. City of Louisville:*

This is an appeal from a judgment upholding the validity of an ordinance of the City of Louisville, Kentucky, which prohibited horseback riding upon public ways and park property (with certain exceptions) in the City of Louisville and which dismissed appellant's claim for an injunction to prohibit the city from interfering with their alleged right to ride horses upon the public ways of the city and in particular upon and along a bridle path located on Southern Parkway.

Appellants' brief assaults the ordinance as being discriminatory in that it applies only to horses as follows:

". . . We, therefore, assume that kangaroo riders can employ bridle paths for their purposes but horse riders cannot. An elephant can be ridden on the bridle path, but a horse cannot. If a tiger could be trained, it could be ridden. Is a donkey or a jackass a horse? What about a mule? Does this relate to live horses only or does it forbid a child rocking on a hobbyhorse? What about a mechanical horse? Could a merry-go-round be set up? The ordinance forbids none of these but only relates to the valiant steed who is such a major part of Kentucky's heritage. The trial court's finding that this ordinance is not discrimina-

tory because it treats all horse riders the same is mis-
founded. If a horse rider cannot ride his horse but can ride
an animal which is not legally a horse, but similar to a
horse, then the ordinance discriminates against not only
the horse but the horse rider. . . .

"Saddling the descendants of Pegasus, Man O'War,
Traveler, Silver, Dan Patch, Widow Maker, Trigger,
Champion, Black Beauty, Bucephalus, Rosinante, and
Black Bess, to name only a few, with this asinine canon is
to denigrate the legacy of the courser and the charger, the
gigster and the stepper, the hunter and the racer, the
clipper and the cob, the padnag and the palfrey, and ca-
pitulate at last to the gasoline-powered conveyance which
has contributed little to our history but much to our eco-
logical turning point."

The evidence in this case clearly indicated that horseback
riding in areas in which vehicular traffic was heavy presented
a serious safety problem which did not exist with respect to
riders of pigs, goats, cattle, elephants, or kangaroos. Thus
there is a valid basis, relating to horses, and not to other
animals, for treating horses as a separate classification for the
purpose of this ordinance.

We also note that the ordinance does not define the term
"horse." That term is therefore subject to judicial interpretation.

The extent to which the term "horse" could possibly be
extended to other animals by statutory construction and
thus allay the fears of appellants that kangaroo and elephant
riders may go unpunished under the ordinance, and that
donkeys, mules, jackasses, and hobbyhorses may not be
horses in the legal sense, is aptly illustrated in *Regina v.
Ojibway*, 8 *Criminal Law Quarterly* 137 (Toronto 1965), in
which the question presented was whether a pony was a
small bird under the provisions of the Small Birds Act.

Until the matter is squarely presented we decline to pass upon the question of the applicability of the ordinance to riders of mules, goats, cattle, or other animals.

. . . .

The Arkansas Omnibus Repealer

J. R. Poisson v. Etienne d'Avril*
Supreme Court of Arkansas, Opinion delivered April 1, 1968

Appeal from Hot Springs Chancery Court, Burl R. Hutch, Chancellor, reversed.

J.R. Poisson, pro se.

Etienne d'Avril, pro se.

George Rose Smith, Justice.   This case—on the surface a routine suit for specific performance of an oral contract for the sale of land—presents, when probed in depth (as we have probed it), the most far-reaching question ever submitted to this court, perhaps to any court in the English-speaking world. The awesome issue confronting us is that of determining to what extent, if any, the common law and the statute law of this state were set aside and annulled by what we will call the Omnibus Repealer, adopted by the legislature in 1945.

The facts are wholly insignificant. Poisson brought this suit against d'Avril to enforce an oral agreement by which d'Avril sold Poisson forty acres of bottom land in the Hot Springs Mountains. D'Avril, as might be expected, pleaded the Statute of Frauds, insisting that under that statute an oral contract for the sale of land cannot be enforced. But

*Published originally in 22 Arkansas Law Review 724 (1969). Copyright © 1969 by Arkansas Law Review and Bar Association Journal, Inc. Reprinted by permission.

Poisson countered by dropping a judicial bombshell. He alleged that the venerable Statute of Frauds, which was adopted in 1838—soon after Arkansas became a state—had been nullified (along with the rest of our laws) by the Omnibus Repealer of 1945. The learned chancellor, appalled by the enormity of the question presented to him, took the case under advisement and finally delivered an opinion rejecting Poisson's sweeping contention, thereby preserving the status quo pending this appeal. The case has now been submitted to us for final decision.

The Omnibus Repealer was appended to Act 17 of 1945—an otherwise innocuous bit of legislation—and reads as follows: "All laws and parts of laws, and particularly Act 311 of the Acts of 1941, are hereby repealed." Period.

Fundamentally, the Repealer hardly calls for judicial interpretation. The legislature has spoken: plainly, clearly, unmistakably, decisively. "All laws and parts of laws . . . are hereby repealed." Under many prior decisions of this court it is unquestionably our solemn duty to give effect to the General Assembly's magnificently comprehensive command. It will suffice to quote two of our earlier pronouncements of the subject.

"It is a well-settled rule of law that, where the will of the Legislature is clearly expressed, the court should adhere to the literal expression of the enactment *without regard to consequences,* and every construction derived from a consideration of its reason and spirit should be *discarded,* for it is *dangerous* to interpret a statute contrary to its express words, where it is not obvious that the makers meant something different from what they have said." (Italics supplied.) *Walker v. Allred,* 179 Ark. 1104, 20 S.W.2d 116 (1929).

"There are certain elemental rules of construction to be observed in the interpretation of statutes from which we will *not* depart. One is that, where a law is plain and unambiguous, there is no room left for construction, and neither the exigencies of a case nor a resort to extrinsic facts will be permitted to alter the meaning of the language used in the statute. *Even where a literal interpretation of the language used will lead to harsh or absurd consequences,* that meaning cannot be departed from unless the whole of the statute furnishes some other guide." (Italics supplied.) *Cunningham v. Keeshan,* 110 Ark. 99, 161 S.W. 170 (1913).

Our duty is clear. "We shall not," in Churchill's words (nor in anyone else's), "flag or fail." Nonetheless, it does occur to us that the pivotal word "laws" in the Omnibus Repealer is open to two interpretations. On the one hand, giving "laws" a strict construction, it may be said to mean statutes only, leaving all judge-made law unmonkeyed with. On the other hand, the word "laws," if given a broad and liberal connotation, may well encompass the common law as well as the digest of statutes, annotated.

In the study of this question we have devotedly worked our law clerks to the bone and, indeed, have lost some sleep ourselves. As far as our research discloses, no other legislative body has ever taken the bold course of repealing all laws—and parts of laws. The nearest parallel we have been able to find, which is persuasive but not binding, is an observation by the great French[1] essayist Montaigne in Chapter 13 of his essay, *Of Experience:* "I am further of opinion that it would be better for us to have no laws at all than to have them in so prodigious numbers as we have."

After much anxious study we have concluded that the legislature intended for the Omnibus Repealer to apply only to statutes, not to common law. We are simply unable to believe that the General Assembly would do away with

---

[1] As it happens, the parties to this suit are, significantly, French.

judge-made law. That law is obviously too wonderful to be lightly tampered with. In the immortal words of Lord Coke (himself, as it happens, a judge): "Reason is the life of the law; nay, the common law itself is nothing else but reason . . . The law, which is perfection of reason." See Bartlett's *Familiar Quotations*, p. 110 (13th ed., 1955).

In reaching our conclusion we attach much weight to the legislature's use of the plural "laws" rather than the singular "law." Had the act undertaken to repeal "all law," it might well be argued that the intent was to abrogate the common law as well as the statutes. But in the Omnibus Repealer, which gives every indication of careful draftsmanship, the lawmakers were careful to refer to "laws" rather than to "law." Thus it may well be true that the letter "s" in "laws" is the most significant "s" in legal literature. At least, counsel have not cited a more significant "s," nor has our own research disclosed one.

Both reason and authority support our interpretation of the Repealer. It is essential that the common law be preserved if we are to avoid anarchy—that state of society where there is no law. The statutory law is not equally essential. Indeed, it will be found that the statutes which were on the books when the Omnibus Repealer was adopted in 1945 can, for the most part, be spared. This is true simply because the common law, always fluid in nature, will at once seep into the temporary vacancy left by the evaporation of the statutes and keep the ship of state safely on the right track.

Counsel for the appellee make the usual last-ditch arguments that are so frequently heard when a court is called upon to perform its stern duty, despite the demands of expediency and wishy-washiness. All sorts of imaginary perils are conjured up. It is said, for instance, that to give full effect to the Omnibus Repealer (hereinafter called the Omnibus Repealer) will nullify such pillars of government as the sales tax

"I, too, remember Dorothy's battle with the Wicked Witch of the West, counselor, but I'm afraid that has no bearing on the issue at hand."

law and the income tax law, both of which antedated 1945. We daresay, however, that the general public can and will face that catastrophe with that serene equanimity born of courage. Again, it is argued, with a veiled threat, that wholesome recreational activities such as horse racing will be abolished by the Repealer. Not so! In its wisdom the common law permits such contests, prohibiting only the secondary practice of betting on the outcome of the races. We need not extend this opinion by discussing one by one the various bugbears envisaged by counsel's vivid imagination. The truth is that in nearly every instance the purposes served by the Omnibus Repealer are praiseworthy and beneficent. We are calling the act to the attention of the Commissioners on Uniform Laws, who may well be inclined to make similar model legislation available to all the states.

The decree must be reversed.

Harris, C.J., would affirm the decree.

John A. Fogleman, Justice, dissenting. I dissent because I disagree.

Ward, Brown, and Jones, JJ., concur in the dissent.

Byrd, J., disqualified.

. . . .

In an astute analysis of the decision entitled "Legislative and Judicial Dynamism in Arkansas: *Poisson v. d'Avril,*" the editors of the *Arkansas Law Review* summarized some of the unique Arkansas statutes that would be affected by the Omnibus Repealer, including prohibitions against driving blindfolded cattle and operating lunch counters or shooting galleries within a half mile of a Confederate cemetery on any national or Confederate decoration day. While noting that only

one of Arkansas' seven Supreme Court justices joined
the majority opinion, the article summed up the significance of *Poisson v. d'Avril* as follows:

Few cases have ever rocketed forth from appellate courts
to literally stun the English-speaking world, and few have
possessed such sweeping significance for the law of a single
jurisdiction as has the recent Arkansas decision of *Poisson v.
d'Avril*. Overnight, in a manner which might well be successfully emulated in other jurisdictions, this decision of the
Arkansas Supreme Court to apply the clearly expressed intent of the state legislature swept away decades of statutory
effluvia, restored much of the beauty of the common law in
its pristine glory, and eradicated legislative acts which would
literally tear at the vitals of a less gutsy jurisdiction. Legal
scholars now gaze in awe at the magnificent destruction
wrought by the Arkansas legislature and bravely carried out
by the state supreme court. Seldom if ever has such an amaz-
ing display of cerebral prowess and uninhibited vision ema-
nated from any legislative body at any time or in any place.

. . . .

The Oberweiss Will

I am writing of my will mineself that dam lawyir want he
should have too much money, he ask too many answers
about the family. First thing I don't want mine brother
Oscar get a G— D—— thing I got. He is muser. He done
me out of forty dollars 14 years since.

I want it that mine kid sister Hilda get the North Sixtie
Akers of at where I am homing it now. I bet she don't
get that gonoph husband of her to brake 20 akers next plow-
ing. She can't have it if she lets Oscar live on it, I want
I should have it back if she does.

Tell Mamma that $600 she been looking for ten years is buried from the backhouse behind about 10 feet down. She better let little Frederich do the digging and count it when he comes up.

Pastor Lucknitz can have $300 if he kisses the book he won't preach no more dumhead talk about politiks. He should a roof put on the meeting house and the elder should the bills look at.

Mamma should the rest get, but I want it so mine brother Adolph should tell her what not she should do so no more slick Irishers sell her vakom cleaners. They noise like hell and a broom don't cost so much.

I want it that my brother Adolph be my execter and I want it that the judge please make Adolph plenty bond put up and watch him like hell. Adolph is a good business man but only a dumkopf would trust him with a busted pfennig.

I want dam sure that schliemiel Oscar don't nothing get, tell Adolph he can have a hundred dollars if he proves judge, Oscar don't nothing get. That dam sure fix Oscar.
                    Signed: Herman Oberweiss

A number of notable legal authorities, including University of California Law School Dean William Prosser and Watergate Special Prosecutor Leon Jaworski, have reproduced the Oberweiss Will, asserting that it was offered for probate in Anderson County, Texas, in 1934. The county clerk for Anderson County is still besieged with requests for copies of the will. Alas, all requests are denied because the will was never offered for probate. As revealed by Judge Jerry Buchmeyer in the *Texas Bar Journal,* the will was written by Houston attorney Will Sears for a law school banquet entertainment in 1931. Will Sears took special delight in how many lawyers overlooked the "internal evidence" of the spuriousness of the Oberweiss Will:

Herman Oberweiss belonged to a congregation led by a "pastor." While several denominations use this term, Herman was obviously German and therefore would have probably been Lutheran or, possibly, Roman Catholic. But would a member of either denomination (or of several others who use the term "pastor") have referred to his church as a meeting house? Neither Lutherans nor Roman Catholics have "elders" at the congregational level. Presbyterians do, and, on occasion, a Presbyterian minister is addressed as "pastor." But "meeting house"? The term is commonly associated with the Society of Friends, who have no "pastors." Even more to the point, however—Herman had a "pastor"; and therefore could hardly have been Jewish. Yet no one has ever, to my knowledge, wondered why Herman, a well-to-do farmer of German descent, living in an East Texas rural county, would use Yiddish words of execration in speaking of Oscar and Hilda's husband!

. . . .

The Christmas Opinions

Opinion No. 84-1225
Issued by California Attorney General John K.
Van de Kamp.
Authored by Deputy Attorney General Ronald M.
Weiskopf.
A MONSIEUR STOFELES OF CONTRA CREDO COUNTY has requested an Opinion of this office on the following questions:

1. Is it a crime to be in a chimney with a bag full of gifts?

2. What can be done about out-of-state reindeer pulling a sled on a California roof?

3. Does the giving of commands to reindeer constitute the practice of veterinary medicine?

The conclusions are:

1. It may or may not be a crime to be in a chimney with a bag full of gifts.

2. The use of out-of-state reindeer to pull a sled on a California roof does not constitute a crime in California. Therefore, little can be done except clean up afterward.

3. The giving of commands to reindeer does not constitute the practice of veterinary medicine.

Analysis

1. We are presented with a person caught in a chimney with a bag full of gifts and are asked whether that constitutes a crime. We conclude that that determination depends on the facts.

Although burglary is a specific intent crime, the element of intent necessary to sustain a burglary conviction "is rarely susceptible of direct proof and must usually be inferred from all the facts and circumstances disclosed by the evidence." (*People v. Henderson* [1956] 138 Cal.App.2d 505, 509.) In this regard, it has been held that an intent to commit a theft from a building may be inferred from an unlawful entry alone (*People v. Fitch* [1946] 73 Cal.App.2d 825, 827), and the unusualness of the hour is another consideration by which the inference of felonious intent on entry has been supported. (*People v. Swenson* [1938] 28

Cal.App.2d 636, 639 [entry in the room of another at 3 A.M. without permission].) In addition, flight from a scene when apprehended may be considered as tending to prove a consciousness of guilt. (Citing *People v. Kittrelle* [1951] 102 Cal.App.2d 149, 158.) It therefore would be for a jury to weigh the evidence in a particular case, including that relating to a defendant's alibi, to determine whether the person caught in a chimney with merchandise was going up the chimney with loot or going down the chimney with gifts. (*People v. D'Elia* [1946] 73 Cal.App.2d 764, 767.)

2. We are next asked whether using out-of-state reindeer to pull a sled on a roof constitutes a crime in California. We conclude that it does not. Several statutes that might at first appear to apply really do not.

Reindeer (genus *Rangifer*) are *not* bovine animals as are bison and buffalo (see *People v. Spencer* [1975] 52 Cal.App.3d 563, 565) within the meaning of Penal Code section 487, subdivision (3) and 14 California Administrative Code section 671, subdivision (b) (17) (B). Fish and Game Code section 3219 deals only with importation for sale, and, in any event, the transitory bringing of reindeer is not an importation (compare *Brown v. Houston* [1885] 114 U.S. 622, 632–634 with *Railroad Co. v. Husen* [1877], 95 U.S. 465 [Missouri regulation of Texas, Mexican, or Indian cattle]) within the meaning of Fish and Game Code section 3219, to make their transitory use in California subject to the Fish and Game Commission. Regarding Food and Agriculture Code section 23032, subdivision (a), which authorizes the stopping of any conveyance *transporting* any horse, mule, burro, or sheep, they are not covered by that section. In any event, while it is a close question as to whether a roof is a "public thoroughfare" as used in section 23032, the section cannot be used to authorize the stopping of a conveyance which is being *transported by*, as opposed to one transporting, reindeer.

3. Lastly, we are asked whether giving commands to reindeer constitutes the practice of veterinary medicine within the meaning of Business and Professions Code section 4826. We conclude in line with our earlier Opinion at 30 Ops.Cal.Atty.Gen. 111 (1957) that merely giving commands such as "up" and "on" to reindeer, by their names, *does not* constitute the practice of veterinary medicine within the meaning of section 4826. It may, however, establish a defense of diminished capacity, which would otherwise be pertinent to a criminal case, but would not in other situations prevent the Board from taking disciplinary action against the person were he a licensee. (*In Re Fahey*, 8 Cal.3d 842, 850–851, fn.4.) But in the situation presented, we disagree with the conclusion reached in *Kris Kringle v. Bd. of Veterinary Examiners of the State of Virginia*, and conclude that there is no ground for administrative action. Yes, Virginia, there is . . . And so we conclude.

. . . .

The impact of antitrust laws on the distribution scheme utilized by Santa and his elves was considered by Oregon Attorney General Dave Frohnmayer, who released the following opinion letter on December 23, 1982:

Mr. S. T. Nicholas
1225 N. Pole
Gnome, Alaska 90001

Dear Mr. Nicholas:

This letter is to inform you of our decision in the complaint of improper business practices brought against you by Mr. I. M. Grinch.

In his complaint, Mr. Grinch has requested that the Oregon Department of Justice immediately seek a temporary restraining order prohibiting you from any business-related activities because of the following alleged violations of state and federal antitrust laws:

1. That by conspiring with parents you cause confusion or misunderstanding as to the source, sponsorship, and approval of your goods and services (ORS 646.608);

2. That by consulting with parents on gifts for children you have furnished them with privileged customer information;

3. That by inciting parents to whisper among themselves and hide presents during the month of December, and by compiling a list and checking it twice, you engage in conspiratorial practices (ORS 646.725);

4. That by discriminating against naughty persons you have accorded special service to some customers in violation of ORS 646.080, which states that customers must be treated on proportionally equal terms;

5. That by linking the receipt of your gifts to persons' good behavior you violated Oregon law which prohibits making product sales conditional upon other behavior;

6. That by giving away presents you have violated federal minimum price regulations;

7. That by claiming to deliver presents all over the world in only one night you are promising delivery of goods

while knowing you are not able to fulfill that promise (ORS 646.607 and 646.608);

8. That you have conspired with Saint Nick, Santa Claus, Père Noel, and others to engage in an illegal restraint of trade by allocating markets and customers and by fixing prices (ORS 646.725); and

9. That you have received kickbacks from your reindeer.

Finally, Mr. Grinch has accused you of having violated ORS 646.730, which states:

> Every person who shall monopolize, or attempt to monopolize, or combine or conspire with any other person or persons to monopolize, any part of trade or commerce, shall be violation of ORS 136.617, 646.705 to 646.805, and 646.990.

We find that you have participated in monopoly, but only in the delivery of the game to children; a non-citable practice.

We conclude that the allegations are unfounded and see no reason to convene a special grand jury. We have, however, filed a counterclaim on your behalf against I. M. Grinch under state antitrust laws for contriving a shortage of good will. His action may also constitute the crime of malicious rottenness.

Further, I have instructed our Consumer Protection Section to pay close attention to enforcement of chimney cleaning regulations for the remainder of 1982.

Merry Christmas,

DAVE FROHNMAYER
Attorney General

DF:tlg

. . . .

The Alfred Packer Legend

Alfred Packer was convicted of murdering his companions in the mountains of Colorado and consuming their flesh while stranded in a blizzard in the winter of 1873. His alleged sentencing by Judge Melville B. Gerry was widely reported in contemporary newspaper accounts:

Stand up, you man-eating son of a bitch, and receive your sentence!

There were seven Democrats in Hinsdale County, but you, you voracious, man-eating, son of a bitch, you ate five of them. I sentence you to be hanged by the neck until you're dead, dead, dead, as a warning against reducing the Democratic population of Hinsdale County. Packer, you Republican cannibal, I would sentence you to Hell but the statutes forbid it.

It makes a good story, but this sentencing never took place. Alfred Packer was very real, however, and so was his crime. In the summer of 1989, law professor James Starrs of George Washington University led an expedition to exhume the bodies of Packer's five victims.

Packer was tried twice for his crimes. At his first trial, he was convicted of murder and sentenced to death. The Colorado Supreme Court reversed the conviction, and he was retried on the lesser charge of manslaughter. After taking the stand in his own defense—and delivering what was described in newspaper accounts as

a "rambling," "wild," and "incoherent" statement—
Packer was convicted of killing his five comrades and
sentenced for forty years in the state penitentiary. All
told, he was a model prisoner, busying himself making
rope and bridles out of hair, before being paroled by the
governor on January 10, 1901.

Packer died in 1907, and was buried in the town
cemetery at Littleton, Colorado. In subsequent years,
Al Packer has become something of a legend. Students
at the University of Colorado have named a University
cafeteria after him, and his contribution to American
cuisine is commemorated by a plaque behind the bar of
the National Press Club in Washington, D.C.

. . . .

TABLE OF CASES

Selmon v. Hasbro Bradley, Inc., 669 F. Supp. 1267 (S.D.N.Y. 1987).

Shafer v. A.A.F.E.S., 667 F. Supp. 414 (N.D.Tex. 1985).

Smith v. Simpson, 648 P.2d 677 (Colo. Ct. App. 1982).

Southeastern Greyhound Corp. v. Graham, 69 Ga. App. 621, 26 S.E.2d 371 (Ga. Ct. App. 1943).

Southeastern Fidelity Ins. Co. v. Fluellen, 128 Ga. App. 877, 198 S.E.2d 407 (Ga. Ct. App. 1973).

Spruance v. Comm'n. on Jud. Qualif., 13 Cal. 3d 778, 532 P.2d 1209, 119 Cal. Rptr. 841 (1975).

State v. Dellinger, 73 N.C. App. 685, 327 S.E.2d 609 (N.C. Ct. App. 1985).

State v. Howery, 204 Mont. 417, 644 P.2d 1387 (1983).

State v. Nelson, 465 N.E.2d 1391 (Ind. 1984).

State v. Strickland, 42 Md. App. 357, 400 A.2d 451 (Md. Ct. Spec. App. 1979).

State v. Woodley, 306 Or. 458, 760 P.2d 884 (1988).

State v. Richter, 36 S.W.2d 954 (Mo. Ct. App. 1931).

United States v. Beltempo, 675 F.2d 472 (2nd Cir. 1982).

United States v. Birdsell, 775 F.2d 645 (5th Cir. 1985).

United States v. Byrnes, 644 F.2d 107 (2nd Cir. 1981).

United States v. Sentovich, 677 F.2d 834 (11th Cir. 1982).

United States v. Widgery, 636 F.2d 200 (8th Cir. 1980).

United States ex rel. Mayo v. Satan & His Staff, 54 F.R.D. 282 (W.D.Pa. 1971).

Vaccaro v. Stephens, 879 F.2d 866 (9th Cir. 1989).

Wheat v. Fraker, 107 Ga. App. 318, 130 S.E.2d 251 (Ga. Ct. App. 1963).

Williams v. State, 126 Ga. App. 350, 190 S.E.2d 785 (Ga. Ct. App. 1972).

Zenith Radio Corp. v. Matsushita Elec. Indus. Co., 478 F.Supp. 889 (E.D.Pa. 1979).

Other Sources

Bishop, *Name-Calling: Defendant Nomenclature in Criminal Trials,* 4 Ohio N.U.L. Rev. 38 (1977).

Buchmeyer, *The Oberweiss Will,* 45 Tex. Bar J. 145 (1982).

Cohen, *A Study in Epithetical Jurisprudence,* 41 L.A. Bar Bull. 374 (June 1966).

Currie, *The Most Insignificant Justice: A Preliminary Consideration,* 50 U. Chi. L. Rev. 466 (1983).

Dox, *Beasts at the Bar,* 4 Lincoln L. Rev. 1 (Jan. 1931).

Easterbrook, *The Most Insignificant Justice: Further Evidence,* 50 U. Chi. L. Rev. 481 (1983).

Note, *Legislative and Judicial Dynamism in Arkansas:* Poisson v. d'Avril, 22 Ark. L. Rev. 724 (1969).

Williams, *The Problems of Long Criminal Trials, A Panel Discussion,* 34 F.R.D. 155, at 184 (Sept. 25, 1963).